EVERY TRICK IN THE BOOK

Over 500 Tricks, Tips, and Tidbits For Quilters

D0957202

By Ami Simms

Illustrations by Julie Hussar

MALLERY PRESS
Flint, Michigan

For Jennie and Steve

Library of Congress Cataloging in Publication Data
Simms, Ami, 1954-
   Every trick in the book / by Ami Simms; illustrated by Julie Hussar.
   p.   cm.
   ISBN 0-943079-02-0
   1. Quilting.   2. Patchwork.   I. Title.
TT835.S53 1990   746.9'7—dc20   89-13867
                                                    CIP

ACKNOWLEDGEMENTS

I am indebted to my fellow quilters for sharing their expertise and ingenuity with me. This book could not have been written without their generosity. I am also most grateful to my family for their support and encouragement during this project, and for their patience and understanding during those times when passion and enthusiasm for things "quilty" force me over that fine line between normal person and obsessed fanatic.

I also wish to thank Michael Gruskin, for his very sound advice; Mary Schafer, for sharing her collection of quilting books and magazines with me; Lois K. Ide for allowing me to reproduce one of her original quilting motifs to illustrate her handy trick; New Pages, Word Crafters, Computer Resource, Inc., CompuTec Typesetting, Inc., and Mico Graphics and Advertising for their superb technical assistance; and the friendly people at Children's Palace, Chimco Prints, Davison Fabrics, Donovan-Mayotte Catholic School, Flint Blueprint Supply, Flint Public Library, Hurley Medical Center, Insty-Prints of Flint, Inc., JD Color Lab, Meijer Pharmacy, Nancy J's Fabric, Pope Glass, Quality Ace Hardware, Rider's Hobby Shop, and Soroc Products, Inc. who provided thoughtful answers to my sometimes silly questions, let me use their facilities, or simply by their dedication, expertise, and professionalism made my job so much easier.

And, finally, special thanks to the editors and publishers of the following books and magazines who granted me permission to use material from their publications: *Canada Quilts*, Chilton Book Company, *Country Needlecraft, Craft Art Needlework Digest, Creative Quilting, Lady's Circle Patchwork Quilts, Patchwork Patter, Quilt, Quilt Almanac, Quilt World, Quilt World Omnibook, Quilter's Newsletter Magazine*, Quilter's Ranch Dispatch, Quilting Today, Quilting USA*, and *Sew News*.

Many thanks to all who helped!

*Note regarding the tricks attributed to *Quilter's Newsletter Magazine* No. 100, No. 200, and to *QNM's Reader Service Leaflet* No. 9: These tips were published by *QNM* prior to their appearance in these three sources. The reader service leaflet and the article "200 Top Tips" in *QNM* Issue No. 200 and the article "100 Top Tips" in *QNM* Issue No. 100 were collections of tips published since 1969 in the magazine. These tricks are included in this book with permission of Leman Publications, Inc.

PREFACE

I've been pumping my own gas at the self-serve island ever since gasoline prices went crazy in 1975. I remember when service station attendants used to do it for me, and fondly recall watching as they would insert the nozzle, start the pump, adjust the handle, and walk over to wash the windshield and check my oil. I now pride myself on being able to do these things all by myself. The transition, however, was not easy. Not wanting to appear stupid, I watched how it was done, imitated what I saw, and pretended that I knew what I was doing. I advanced slowly. (This is very similar to the way I learned to quilt.)

Until a short time ago, I assumed mastery of the self-serve pump was limited to being able to wrestle the hose all the way over to the tank opening instead of attempting to fill the thing through the fender, and squeezing the handle hard enough and long enough to fill the entire tank. I thought if I could do this in sub-zero Michigan winters, at stations with ugly signs that say "PAY FIRST," and without spilling gasoline on my shoes, I was doing all right.

Recently I discovered a little metal latch on the handle of the pump that can be flipped to hold the handle in the "on" position. Once it is set the gas flows *all by itself* until the tank is full. Then it flops back into place, releasing the handle and stopping the gas! I cannot tell you the joy I experienced in discovering this little tidbit.

I no longer ride around on the fumes hoping that Steve will take pity on me and fill the tank for me. I no longer feel like a slave chained to the handle of the gas pump, my hand fusing into a semi-permanent flexed position, until the tank gurgles and says it's had enough.

Now I set the lever and do things I never dreamed of doing. I walk around the car and kick the tires. I lift the hood and look for the dipstick. (One of these days I'm going to find it!) I crawl in the nice warm car and watch the numbers on the pump click by *from the inside*. It's a very small thing, but it has changed my life! (OK, so maybe it hasn't changed my life, but it sure has changed the way I pump gas!)

Compiling the tips for *Every Trick In The Book* has changed the way I make quilts. The book contains over 500 "new" ways to solve old problems. Some were old friends, others were as revolutionary as the little lever on the gasoline pump.

Obviously not all the tricks can be for every quilter. Some tricks are very narrow in focus, some are contradictory, and others are redundant! Still, they all offer valid options. And they bring to light the resourcefulness and creativity of the quilting community.

Every Trick In The Book began in early 1987 with a list of my favorite tricks and letters to some of the larger quilting guilds enlisting their help with the project. Quilters on the "workshop circuit" were asked to contribute, tricks were solicited from my students, and a search of the quilting literature was begun. It took just over three years to gather, organize, and document the information.

My intention was to give due credit for each trick whenever possible. This, however, was easier said than done. Many of the tricks are so well known it was impossible to discover the original source, if indeed there was just one. Individuals faced with the same problem

often come up with the same solution, independently.
Anthropologists invoke the dictum of independent in-
vention to explain two cultures that progress along similar paths though they have had no contact with one
another. It is applicable here as well. To borrow a more
humorous explanation from Elly Sienkiewicz: "There's a
lot of 'spontaneous combustion' going on!"

Add to that the fact that quilting tricks have been
shared and passed down through generations of
stitchers, usually with much more thought given to the
trick than to its author. While this presents a formi-
dable challenge to the researcher, it speaks highly of
her fellow quilters. Nowhere, it seems, is the spirit of
sharing more alive than in the world of quiltmaking!

Tricks were handled in strict chronological order.
That is, if two or more people submitted the same trick,
the first one submitted was included in the book, the
second (third, fourth, etc.) was not. Similarly, if, in my
perusal of the quilting literature, a trick was found in a
magazine or book that pre-dated the submitted trick,
the magazine was credited. When two different magazines offered the same trick, the magazine with the ear-
liest publication date was cited. Also, as you might
expect, not every trick submitted appears in the book.
You may credit my wisdom or curse my stupidity,
whichever works best for you.

Each trick appearing in *Every Trick In The Book*
has been "footnoted" except those that I contributed.
The "footnotes" appear in sections called Chapter Notes
at the end of each chapter. Since the attribution in
many cases is longer than the trick, I felt it would be
less distracting for the reader if it were handled in this
way. My original notion of putting the name of the con-
tributor in parentheses immediately after the trick
made the text incredibly disjointed and difficult to follow, and was therefore abandoned. The tricks are not

numbered for the same reason. The index therefore lists contributors as well as their tricks.

Every Trick In The Book was great fun to write. The process was both entertaining and informative. By learning new tricks, or rediscovering old ones, I've become a better quilter. I hope that you'll enjoy reading it as much as I enjoyed writing it.

Ami Simms
Flint, Michigan
March 1990

CONTENTS

CHAPTER ONE
FABRIC PREPARATION

Selecting Fabric

When purchasing fabric, buy the very best you can afford. Quality fabric is easier to work with, looks better, will last longer, and is worth your time and money.

Need to remember what's stashed at home before buying another yard? Record yardage on hand, fabric width, fiber content, place of purchase, price, etc. in a small notebook and staple a swatch next to the pertinent information. Bring it to the fabric store.[1]

To see prints more clearly, try a homemade cardboard viewfinder. Cut two holes (1" x 1" and 2" x 2") in a piece of scrap cardboard, making windows through which only small parts of the fabric can be seen at one time. Isolating just a portion of a larger print or overall design will help you see what the fabric would look like sewn into small patches.[2]

When comparing two pieces of fabric of the same weight, remember that thread count isn't the whole story. The number of threads per inch may not be as important as the density or thickness of each thread. Hold each fabric up to the light. The one which allows the least amount of light to penetrate is likely the better fabric for quilting, excluding very tight weaves such as percale.[3]

To examine things a bit more closely, try a magnifying glass or photographer's loupe and take a good look at the weave through a window template. Make this tool by cutting a 1" square out of a piece of graph paper. Place it over the fabric and count the threads in each direction, or simply look for fabric without large "holes."[4]

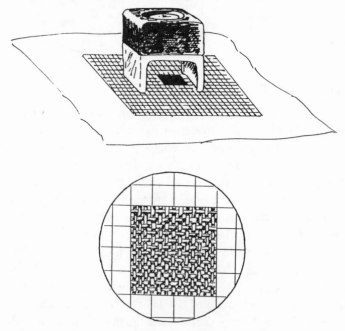

Use a loupe to check fabric weave.

Sometimes your eyes can play tricks on you. Viewing colors in artificial light may not give a true reading. If it is important to see the *real* color of a piece of goods, ask permission to take the bolt outside into natural light. The same fabric may read differently in daylight than in fluorescent or incandescent light.

To see its true color, ask to take the fabric outside.

When buying fabric for a particular project, buy an extra quarter yard of everything. Each time the quilt is washed, throw in the extra yardage at the same time. Should the quilt ever need repair, fabric that *really* matches will be on hand.[5]

Testing For Fiber Content

To determine the fiber content, pull a thread from the fabric and hold it over a small flame with a pair of pliers, tongs, or tweezers. Protein fibers, such as cotton and wool, will emit a gray smoke when burned. They will also leave a small bit of ash residue and will smell like burning hair. Synthetic fibers, such as polyester, will give off a black smoke and leave a shiny black residue. They will smell like burning plastic.[6] It is also possible to iron fabric to determine the fiber content. Fabrics with a high cotton content will take creases better than fabrics with more polyester in them. Generally, the sharper the crease, the more cotton is present.

Another, perhaps less accurate, way to test for fabric content is to smell the piece of fabric as it is ironed. If it smells like plastic, it most likely has synthetic materials in it.[7] Take care that detergents and/or fabric softeners don't confuse the issue.

Washing Fabric

Always pre-wash and dry all fabric used in quilt-making. This will remove sizing put on by the manufacturer, and, most importantly, will allow the fabric to do whatever shrinking it's going to do BEFORE it's sewn into a quilt. This is also a good time to check for color-fastness.

Unfold fabric that has been folded and wound tightly around the bolt before tossing it into the washing machine. This will make the center crease easier to iron out later.

To prevent raveling, fraying, and tangling, cut all raw edges with pinking shears before laundering.[8] Or zigzag the raw edges before washing the fabric.[9] For something a little easier, simply clip a small triangle off each corner.[10] Less fabric will be lost, and it won't take quite as much time. To speed things up even more, fold the fabric in quarters and whack off all four corners at once.

Clip off corners to reduce tangling.

All three methods will indicate which pieces in the closet have been washed and which ones haven't. Another reminder to keep from needlessly washing fabric a second (or third) time is to place a small safety pin in one corner.[11]

Small scraps that need pre-washing can be run through the washer in a mesh lingerie bag on the delicate cycle.[12]

Testing For Colorfastness

Good quality fabric should hold its color after washing. Any excess dye not stabilized during the manufacturing process should come off after a single machine washing. (Some bright or dark colors may require a second wash.) If there is significant color loss after successive machine washings, either find a way to stop the color loss or avoid using the fabric.

To check for color loss, catch a few cups of rinse water in a clear glass container as the water exits the washing machine. Let it stand for a few minutes, then hold it against a white wall or a white piece of paper. If the water is not absolutely clear, there may be a problem. Run the fabric through another rinse (possibly another wash cycle as well) until the rinse water is completely clear.

When washing fabric a second time, toss in a white tea towel. If it comes out white, the fabric is colorfast.[13]

Colorfastness can be checked when the fabric is dry, too. Clip off a small piece and put it in a white dish of hot water. Let it stand at least an hour before removing the fabric. If the water changes color, try washing again and repeat the test.

Wetting the sample piece of fabric with hot water and setting it on white fabric or paper toweling is also a good test. If it dries leaving a stain, try again.

Probably the best test quilters can make is to construct a sample block using the fabrics in question. Either sew them as they will be placed in the actual quilt, or sew any questionable fabrics to muslin, then wash.[14]

"Fixing" Colors

Most fabrics quilters use are dyed with either pigment dyes or rapidogen dyes. In the case of prints, sometimes both are used. Pigment dyes are allowed to dry; rapidogen dyes must be set by means of an acid steam bath. Rapidogen dyes that are not properly set may be responsible for color loss. If so, home remedies which introduce solutions that are slightly acetic to wash water *may* keep fabrics from losing color but are not guaranteed to.[15]

So to stop colors from bleeding, add 1/4 cup salt to the rinse water and let the solution and fabric soak for 15 minutes.[16] Or treat quilting fabric to a final warm water soak with Epsom salt or vinegar to set the colors.[17]

These items may keep some fabrics from bleeding.

Drying Fabric

Before putting wet fabric into the dryer, untangle and clip all loose threads. A small pair of scissors can be kept in the laundry area for this purpose. Then give each piece a good shake to cut down on tangling, creasing, and streaking.

Fabric should be allowed to dry thoroughly before it is removed from the dryer so that it will be completely pre-shrunk. Future surprises can be avoided this way.

Do not dry cotton/polyester blend fabrics in the dryer with fabric softeners that come in sheet form, as they can cause "grease" spots on some fabrics.

Miscellaneous Tips

To remove "drip-dry" or other finishes on cotton fabrics, boil them for 15 minutes in a solution of one part white vinegar to four parts water. This makes the fabric more compatible with those that have no such factory finish.[18]

Fabrics can be "antiqued" by tea-staining them in a solution made from one large tea bag steeped in a gallon of water. Let the fabric soak for about five minutes.[19]

Be sure to wash tea-stained fabric immediately after staining to halt the reaction between the tanic acid and the fabric. Tea-staining is not recommended for quilts receiving lots of use as it weakens the fabric.[20]

Before writing on patches used in friendship, autograph, or signature quilts, stabilize the fabric by pressing the shiny side of a piece of freezer paper to the wrong side of the signature block. Peel it away after the ink dries.[21]

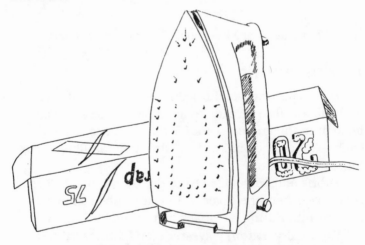

Freezer paper stabilizes fabric.

When signing or inscribing quilts with calligraphy, spray the back of the block with Magic® Sizing Fabric Finish. It is easier to trace through than a block backed with freezer paper, is easy to write on, and noticeably inhibits the ink from bleeding.[22]

Chapter Notes

[1]Pat Nagy, in "Money Savers," *Quilter's Newsletter Magazine*, #67 (May 1975) p. 10.

[2]Mary Conroy: Sudbury, Ontario.

[3]Jeffrey Gutcheon: New York.

[4]Jeffrey Gutcheon, "Fabric Properties: Thread Count, Blends & Finishes," *Quilter's Newsletter Magazine Reader Service Leaflet #13*, 1985.

[5]"100 Top Tips," *Quilter's Newsletter Magazine*, #100 (March 1978) p. 12.

[6]"The Burn Test," *Quilter's Newsletter Magazine*, #186 (October 1986) p. 49.

[7]Ibid. p. 49.

[8]"100 Top Tips," *Quilter's Newsletter Magazine Reader Service Leaflet #9*, 1984.

[9]Rosalie Pfeifer, in "Tip For Fabric Collectors," *Quilter's Newsletter Magazine*, #179 (February 1986) p. 41.

[10]Paul McDade: Hamilton, OH.

[11]Elly Sienkiewicz, in "Top Tips," *Quilter's Newsletter Magazine*, #203 (June 1988) p. 48.

[12]"200 Top Tips," *Quilter's Newsletter Magazine*, #200 (March 1988) p. 10.

[13]Pat Morris: Glassboro, NJ.

[14]Jeffrey Gutcheon, "Fabric Properties: Color Loss And Cleaning," *Quilter's Newsletter Magazine Reader Service Leaflet #12*, 1985.

[15]Jeffrey Gutcheon, "Not For Shopkeepers Only," *Quilter's Newsletter Magazine*, #185 (September 1986) p. 62.

[16]Rosalie Pfeifer, in "Tip For Fabric Collectors," *Quilter's Newsletter Magazine*, #179 (February 1986) p. 41.

[17]Virginia Avery, as cited by Jeffrey Gutcheon, "Fabric Properties: Color Loss And Cleaning," *Quilter's Newsletter Magazine Reader Service Leaflet #12*, 1985.

[18]Mary Conroy: Sudbury, Ontario.

[19]*Quilt*, Winter 1988, p. 21.

[20]Judy Anne Walter: Evanston, IL.

[21]*Greater San Antonio Quilt Guild Newsletter*, 1987, as cited in *Trinity Valley Quilter's Guild Newsletter*, Vol. 6, No. 7, p. 9.

[22]Elly Sienkiewicz: Washington, D.C.

CHAPTER TWO
COLOR AND DESIGN

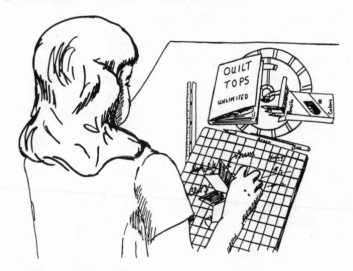

Getting Ideas

Pictures of quilts made by other artists are a great
source of inspiration. Post cards, snapshots, and magazine clippings can be organized for easy retrieval in plastic page protectors which have an opening at the top.
They can hold lots of pictures, and most come with
holes punched at the side so that they can be stored in
three-ring binders.[1]

Inexpensive photo albums with the peel-back pages
are handy, too.[2] Use a magnifying glass for a closer
look.[3]

Children's coloring books provide another source of
inspiration, especially for those inclined toward applique. Shapes are drawn simply and are easily adapted
to cloth.[4] Cookie cutters work well, too, and they're already in template form![5]

When the work of another inspires you to create a
quilt, DO credit the original artist and mention the

source of your design when you share your work with others.

Getting Them To Size

Keep the measurements of all the beds in your home in a notebook or some other handy place. No need to waste valuable time re-measuring the same bed twice. Or three times![6]

A pantograph will enlarge or reduce a block to fit any design scheme. They are available at art supply stores where drafting tools are sold.

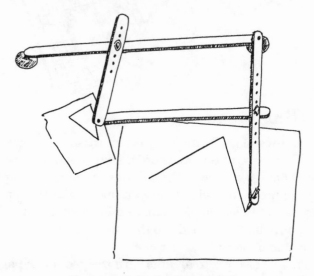

Pantographs enlarge or reduce.

Patchwork designs can be drawn to size by using an opaque projector, too. Photographs, books, and sketches can be projected in almost any size onto paper taped to the wall and traced line for line. If inspiration comes in slide form, a simple slide projector will do the trick. Check schools or libraries for these machines. In larger cities, they can also be rented.

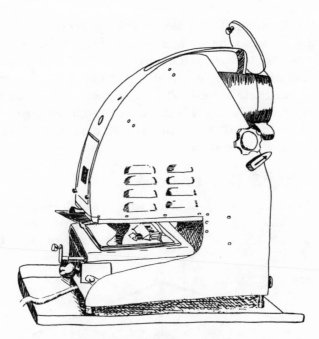

An opaque projector can scale images up or down.

If all this seems like too much trouble, try the local printer. Many offset or "quick" printers have copy machines for small jobs that will enlarge and reduce, as well as reproduce an exact image. They're perfect for quilting patterns and quilting motifs, as long as the original is small enough to fit in the machine. If the image is too large, fold it or cut it apart to fit, then tape the resulting copies back together again like a jigsaw puzzle.

Some machines may distort the image, if only slightly, so do a sample run first. Place the copy over the original and hold it up to a bright light. If lines match up horizontally *and* vertically, the machine makes accurate copies.[7] If they don't, and precision work is the goal, lines may need to be re-drawn and proportions checked again. Or find another copy machine.

For the ultimate in painless enlargement, have someone else do the work! Small copy shops can put their camera to work and enlarge up to 11" x 17". Commercial printers may go up as high as 20" x 30". Large commercial printing establishments, especially those in big cities, may be able to offer photographic enlargements up to 4' x 6', but cameras with a capacity of this size are not very common.

Getting A Better Look

If you have one quilt block with possibilities but need to know what two blocks in the same pattern would look like, hold a pocket mirror at a right angle to the block.

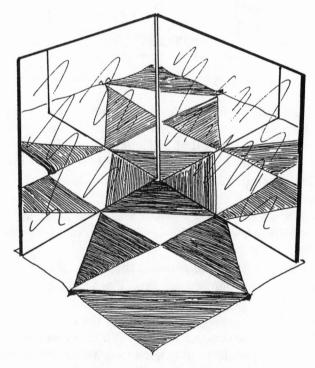

Mirrored ceiling tiles repeat the design.

Two 12" mirrored ceiling tiles, taped together at
right angles and placed around one quilt block, will reflect the image of the block so that it appears as though
there are four. Three mirrored tiles will reflect the
image indefinitely to show what the entire quilt might
look like.[8]

A multi-lens reflector, available at most office or art
supply stores, will show one block through 25 rectangu-
lar lenses, all at the same time![9]

Interested in seeing what a border design will look
like turning the corner? Hold a hand mirror at a 45°
angle against the design for a pretty good idea.[10]

Need something more tangible? Head back to the
copy shop. Copy the block as many times as necessary,
and tape the images together. It sure beats sketching
the same block a dozen or more times. After they've
been taped, make a copy of the copies for easy han-
dling. And, while the machine is still running, make a
few extra copies to experiment with different color
schemes, using colored markers, pencils, or crayons.[11]

When working with complicated patterned fabrics,
especially stripes, photocopying the *fabric* can be a big
help. Use the "paper fabric" to make a paper mock-up
of the quilt before cutting into the *real* cloth. Hopefully,
all mistakes will be made on the paper, painlessly.[12]

Visually isolating big prints or busy fabric can be a
problem. Make a window template out of opaque plastic
template material, the same size as the finished patch,
and move it over the fabric. It will show what the patch
will look like once it is sewn.[13]

Finding Value And Contrast

When selecting fabrics, value and contrast are as
important as color. A simple yet effective way to check
value (the relative lightness or darkness), is to place the
fabrics under consideration side by side in a poorly lit

room. Squint your eyes almost shut until the fabric is
just barely visible. Patterns of light and dark become
more dominant than color, and subtle gradations of
values are more obvious. If this is difficult, place the
fabric in a darkened room equipped with a rheostat.
Slowly adjust the rheostat, increasing the amount of
light until the value is noticeable, but not the color. If
you can tolerate another trip to the copy shop, photo-
copy the fabric again, this time to check value and contrast without the distraction of color.[14]

Getting It Together

Fabric mock-ups offer a great opportunity to test options. Spray adhesives create a slightly tacky surface
on which to position and re-position fabric patches for
experimentation with color, contrast, and pattern.[15]

Self-adhesive shelf paper, sticky side up on a draw-
ing board, is also a good surface on which to play with
cut fabric pieces without losing any. The tackiness of
the paper will hold everything in place as various design options are considered. Keep the paper in place
with masking tape all the way around the edges.[16]

A piece of felt also provides a slightly clingy surface
on which to plan quilts. Patches can be pinned to it or
just positioned on it. They'll stay in place for a surprisingly long time, provided they're not set near an open
window. Felt is also handy for large scale mock-ups
and for assessing a quilt in progress. Just put the
patches on the felt, stand back, and admire the view.[17]

Cotton flannel, some kinds of quilt batting, and
needle punched interfacing will also provide a place to
display work in progress. Tack it to a sheet of plywood
or directly to the wall.[18] Or pin patches to large sheets
of styrofoam.[19]

For something more substantial, 4' x 8' insulation
boards can be covered with felt, flannel, or muslin and

mounted on the wall. The covering will be slightly clingy, and the insulation board will accept pins, too.[20]

For something less permanent and more portable, stretch the flannel around an artist's canvas and staple. The canvas can balance on push pins or small nails in the wall and can be removed or re-positioned easily. The size and configuration is negotiable.[21]

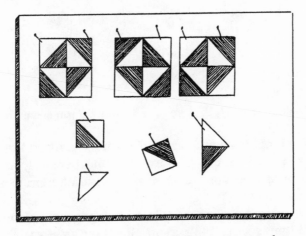

Position and re-position patches as you work.

Pinning or placing quilt patches or blocks in progress on a quilt already on display works in a pinch, but only if the pattern of the finished quilt doesn't distract from viewing the work in progress.

Enjoying The View

Backing up and squinting is probably the best way to see how colors and shapes are coming together. The farther back, the more accurate the overall picture. If standing back far enough to really *see* the work isn't possible, look at it through a camera lens or a reducing lens.[22] Gazing through the wrong end of a pair of binoculars will also help.[23]

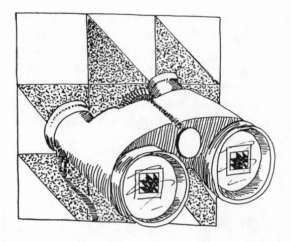

Looking through the *wrong* end can help you see more!

Looking through a peep hole is handy, too.[24] Peep holes, sans door, can be purchased inexpensively at most hardware stores and make a great addition to any sewing basket.

Viewing the same work in a photograph may show more than seeing it in person. Shoot quilts at various stages of their construction with an instant camera to see three dimensions reduced to two in a matter of seconds. Save the photographs for a permanent record of the changes made as the work progresses. Alternatives can be compared easily, and subtle changes won't be forgotten.[25]

Chapter Notes

[1] Sharyn Craig: San Diego, CA.

[2] Susan Meindl: Kent, OH.

[3] Marjorie Fetterhoff, *Quilter's Ranch Dispatch*, January/February 1987, p. 7.

[4] Anne Wittels, "Granny Sez," *Quilt World*, July/August 1981, p. 22.

[5] Katherine M. Barnhill, in "Top Tips," *Quilter's Newsletter Magazine*, #20 (June 1971) p. 12.

[6]Kay Burns, "Quilt-Words To The Quilt Wise: Ten Best Quilting Tips," *Quilt*, Spring 1989, p. 67.

[7]Debbie Hall, "Paper Sewn Triangles," *American Quilter*, Spring 1988, p. 51.

[8]Judy Mathieson: Woodland Hills, CA, as told to her by a student.

[9]Jean Pell, "Tools Of The Trade," *Quilt World*, September/October 1982, p. 45.

[10]Louise Townsend, "Easy Quiltmaking Lesson #133," *Quilter's Newsletter Magazine*, #159 (February 1984) p. 22.

[11]"200 Top Tips," *Quilter's Newsletter Magazine*, #200 (March 1988) p. 11.

[12]Barbara Brackman: Lawrence, KS.

[13]Judith Montano: Castle Rock, CO.

[14]John H. Rust: Hilton Head Island, SC.

[15]Judy B. Dales: Boonton Township, NJ.

[16]David Pottinger, "Helpful Hints From Indiana Quilters," *Lady's Circle Patchwork Quilts*, February/March 1987, p. 62.

[17]Donna Maki: Holt, MI.

[18]Nancy Dice: Bellevue, WA.

[19]Betty Gavere, "A Light In The Dark," *Quilt World*, September/October 1987, p. 64.

[20]Mary Mashuta: Berkeley, CA.

[21]Nancy Dice: Bellevue, WA, as told to her by a friend.

[22]Nancy Dice: Bellevue, WA.

[23]Jean V. Johnson: Olathe, KS. Shared by Peggy Greene: Indianapolis, IN.

[24]Katie Pasquini: Oxnard, CA.

[25]Jane Hall: Raleigh, NC. Shared by Sonja Shogren: Raleigh, NC.

CHAPTER THREE
DRAFTING

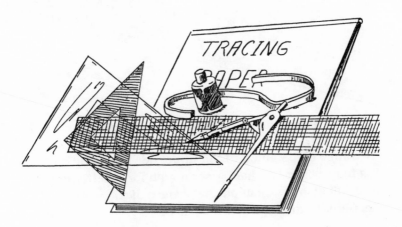

Drafting Tools

To insure accuracy while drafting, use the same ruler from start to finish. Not all rulers are the same, and even the slightest discrepancy can throw things off. Check also to see that the ruler isn't warped or worn at the ends. If it is worn, start measuring at the 1" mark instead of at the end.[1]

Some rulers, the clear plastic kind, come with their own quarter-inch grid. They are especially handy when adding seam allowances to pattern pieces.[2] If your clear plastic ruler is without such a grid, 1/4" masking tape will work in a pinch, although it may need replacing from time to time.

Peanut butter smeared onto plastic rulers will remove gummy residues left over from masking tape and other adhesives.[3]

If you have a problem picking up flat plastic rulers and right triangles, try a plastic suction cup (the kind used to hang "sun catchers" on windows) as a handle.[4]

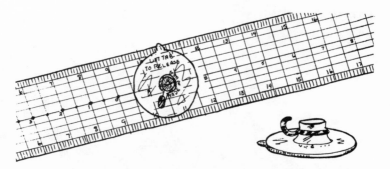

Plastic suction cups make great handles.

Bingo chips glued to the underside of plastic drafting tools will raise them just enough for a better grip
and will also lift them off the surface of the paper to
keep ink from seeping under them.[5]

Drafting Squares

Floor tiles are ready-made, perfectly square, 12"
templates. Manufacturers also make smaller tiles for 9"
templates.[6] Use floor tiles to cut out batting for quilt-as-
you-go projects.[7]

Want to turn squares on point? To find the precise
diagonal measurement of any square, multiply the side
by 1.414235. Or to get "close enough," divide the side
of the square by 2.4, and then add the side of the
square to the quotient.[8] For example, to find the diagonal of a 12" square either multiply (12" x 1.414235 =
16.97") or divide and then add (12" ÷ 2.4 = 5" then 5" +
12 = 17").

Drafting Circles

A good compass should be standard sewing equip-
ment. Pulling the compass legs apart to get the right
size circle sure beats rummaging through the kitchen
in search of the right sized plate, pot, or pan.

When a standard compass is too small, large circles and arcs can be roughly sketched with a push pin, a length of string, and a pencil. Use the push pin to anchor one end of the string in the middle of the circle, and tie the other end of the string around the pencil an appropriate distance away. Holding the pencil perpendicular to the paper, move it carefully around the push pin or slide the paper under the pencil.

See-through plastic rulers (the kind with the red lines) sometimes come with holes drilled down the middle. Stick a pin in one hole, a pencil in another, and rotate the pencil and ruler around the pin. It's a lot more accurate.

Larger circles can be made using the same principle. Drill small holes at one inch increments down the center of a wooden yardstick. Place the last hole at the center of the circle and secure with a push pin or tack. Put the pencil point in the appropriate hole, and pivot around the pin.[9]

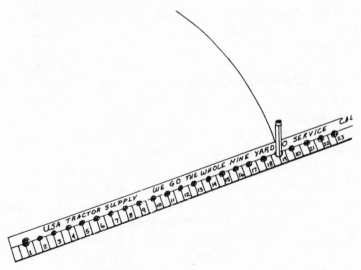

A makeshift compass.

For accurate circles drawn exactly to size, not the closest hole in the yardstick, try a yardstick compass. It's completely adjustable, and will make circles up to 72" in diameter using a standard yardstick. They can be found at most art supply stores and well-stocked quilt shops. Yardstick sold separately.

Drafting Strategies

Combining circles and squares? When making templates for curved blocks, like Drunkard's Path, think about hand piecing the curves and machine piecing the straight seams. Make templates *without* the seam allowance on the curved edges and *with* the seam allowance on the straight edges. (Notches along the curved seams will help in placement.) When laying the templates on the fabric, leave room to add the seam allowance on the curved edges when cutting. This does not need to be done for the straight edges, as the seam allowance has already been incorporated. In drafting the templates this way, the edge of the template represents the cutting line on the straight edges and the sewing line on the curves.[10]

When hand piecing, window templates can be made for marking sewing and cutting lines at the same time. First draw the finished size (without seam allowances), then measure 1/4" all around and mark the second line. Using a craft knife or razor blade, cut on the inside line first, then on the outside line.[11]

For more accurate machine piecing, trim any template corners sharper than 90° according to your piecing strategy. By lopping off corners that extend beyond the 1/4" seam allowance, at the angle at which they meet neighboring patches, perfect alignment with very little fuss can be achieved. Create the templates first, then think of the order in which they will be sewn. Place the first template over the second, as if they were the actual patches about to be sewn, and trim the first template to fit the second. (In some instances, the second template will also need to be trimmed to fit the first.) Continue fitting the templates together and trimming corners that extend too far until the entire block has been analyzed.[12]

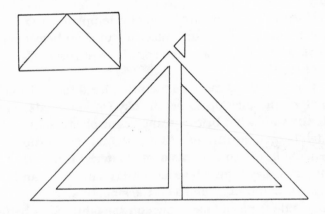

Trimming template points ensures accuracy.

Template Material

For non-repeat or few-repeat templates, try lightweight to medium non-woven interfacing. Cut the pattern out of the interfacing, then pin it to the fabric as if it were a dress pattern. This method is faster than cutting rigid templates, and storage is easy, too. Just pin them all to the master pattern for the next time.[13]

Cardboard has always been a perennial favorite for templates because it seems to be so handy. Most any empty box around the house will work, provided it's big enough to get the entire template out without cutting on the folds. Since it's opaque, pattern pieces from books and magazines will have to be glued directly to it, or traced onto another piece of paper first, and then glued.

When gluing patterns made from thin paper to thick cardboard, spray adhesive will give an even coat without the globs and mess of glue sticks or water-based glues.[14]

To keep the edges of cardboard templates from wearing with successive tracings, reinforce the edges with tape.[15]

Manila file folders are handy for templates, too. They are easy to draw on, easier to cut than heavy cardboard, and will hold a sharp edge for a surprisingly long time.[16]

For something more substantial, head to the local toy store and pick up some Shrinky Dinks™. Kids decorate the somewhat brittle, translucent plastic material, which is then shrunk to 1/3 its original size in the oven. Quilters can use this same material for making templates. Lay it directly over patterns in books and magazines and mark lines on the smooth side. The rough side is placed face down on the fabric for a better grip. This "template material" is also sold separately in refill packages. Keep it away from hot irons, for obvious reasons.[17]

Another good template substitute is spoiled x-ray film from the local hospital or clinic. Sometimes x-ray films are unusable because the wrong setting was used, jewelry was inadvertently left on the patient, or the patient moved, making the x-ray too blurry to read. Before the wasted films are sold (the silver used in developing the x-ray can be recovered) they are fair game for quilters bold enough to beg a few pieces.[18] If you don't mind someone's bones on your Bear's Paw, you're all set.

Generally several layers stapled or glued together provide the right thickness. Or they can be glued or stapled to cardboard. They will not wear down with successive tracings and can be easily marked.

Spent x-ray films make good templates.

Plastic lids from margarine tubs and coffee cans make sturdy templates. They're easy to see through and to cut.[19] Plastic bleach bottles[20] and milk bottles[21] make good template material, too. Cut off the tops and bottoms, slice them along one side so they will lie flat, and place them under a weight in a dish pan of hot water for about 20 minutes. Dry, then place under a pile of books for 24 hours.[22]

The plastic insert in some bacon packages can also be used as template material. Be sure to wash it thoroughly.[23] And linoleum scraps make templates that are nearly indestructible. They are best cut at room temperature with a strong hand.[24]

Lexan™, a heavy duty plastic manufactured in a variety of thicknesses for use in everything from motorcycle helmet visors to bullet-proof windows, can also be used for templates.[25] Only the thinnest sheets, however, can be cut with a pair of scissors. There are many other plastics on the market which can be used for making templates, too. Check the local hobby shop or plastics manufacturer/distributor.

Writing On Template Material

To make plastic template edges easier to see, lay them on a piece of scrap paper and run a large, permanent, wide tip marker along the edge of the template.[26]

Write the name of the quilt, finished block size, how many of each color to cut, grainline, and any other pertinent information on the smooth side of each template. It will keep the template from getting lost, and will remind you to use it rough side down.

Narrow line permanent ink felt tip pens are easier to use on slippery template material than ordinary pencils or ball point pens. The line stays put, dries quickly, doesn't smear, and won't skip. They come in a variety of widths and colors.[27] Grease pencils will also give a good dark line, but they're hard to sharpen.

If suitable marking pens are not available, use what's handy and hope that it stays on long enough to cut the template accurately. If markings on the face of the template look as if they might smear, cover them with transparent tape.[28]

Take full advantage of plastic template material when working with stripes and large patterned fabrics that will be placed the same way each time the patch appears in the block. After marking the first piece, trace the stripe or pattern directly onto the plastic template. It will be much easier to match the fabric the next time.[29]

Cutting Templates

It's a good idea to have a pair of scissors specifically for cutting templates, especially if linoleum is the template material of choice. Mark the scissors, even if they are not the same brand and style, to distinguish them from scissors used for cutting fabric. Red nail polish or a snippet of yarn tied to the handle should do the trick.

Keep two rotary cutters on hand. Use one cutter for fabric, the other for templates. Fill the second cutter with old blades from the first.[30] If template material is sliding around on your cutting mat, tape it to the mat and hold it securely as you cut.[31]

Paper cutters will also slice most template material leaving a sharp, smooth edge. Line up one side of the template against the top of the paper cutter and the other side against the right edge for a perfect right angle.[32]

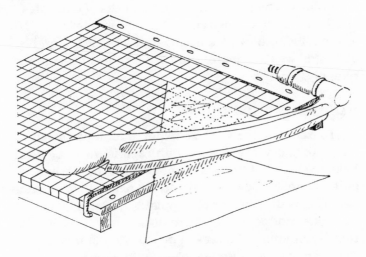

Paper cutters cut templates, too.

Creating Non-Skid Templates

Commercial template material now comes with a non-skid surface on one side. The smooth side faces up so that it can be written on, and the rough side faces down on the fabric for more traction.

A non-skid template can be made by gluing a layer of fine sandpaper to the back of any template. If that seems too wasteful, just glue small narrow strips of sandpaper instead. Or use double-sided tape to affix the sandpaper.[33]

For small projects that do not require much tracing, skip the template and glue paper patterns directly to the sandpaper.[34]

Hardware stores also sell self-adhesive sandpaper sheets so that the gluing step can be skipped entirely. Just peel back and press.

Or forget the sandpaper and just place a strip of double-sided tape in the center of the template to hold it steady.[35]

Rubber cement brushed on the backs of templates and then allowed to dry keeps them from moving around, too. If they pick up too much fabric lint and don't grip well any more, rub off the rubber cement and re-apply.[36]

Figuring Yardage

To calculate the yardage required for a particular template, follow these steps with each fabric to be used: Take the width of the fabric and divide it by the height of the template. Round down to the nearest whole number. This is the number of templates that can be cut from one width of fabric. Then divide that number into the total number of pieces to be cut. Round that up to the nearest whole number. This is the number of rows, or widths, needed. Multiply the number of rows by the width of the template to get the length of fabric needed in inches. Divide the number of inches by 36 to calculate the number of yards needed.[37]

For example, let's say you've got a 5" x 5" square template, and the pattern calls for 437 of them. To find out how many yards of 44" wide calico to buy, first divide 44" by 5". That's 8.80. Rounding down, it becomes 8. In other words, the template can be traced 8 times from selvage to selvage. Then divide 437 by 8. That's 54.63; rounded up, it becomes 55. Trace 55 rows of 8. Multiply 55 by 5" to get the number of inches of fabric (275"), and divide by 36 to come up with 7.64 yards, or about 7 and 5/8 yards.

If yardages are already given in the pattern, but for the "wrong" width fabric, re-work the math above, or convert the yardages thus: To convert yardages from 36" wide fabric to 45" wide fabric, multiply by .85. To go the other way, multiply by 1.25.[38]

Storing Templates

Nothing is more irritating than having to re-invent the wheel. If there's a chance of using templates more than once, save them. Plastic zippered pouches that fit inside three-ring binders and can help keep templates organized and easy to find. Store them by shape (all triangles together) or by pattern.[39]

Dividers that fit three-ring binders can also be used to organize templates. Put the templates in a re-closable plastic bag and staple it to the divider. Label the divider and store it in the binder.[40]

Re-sealable plastic food storage bags will keep templates and directions from getting misplaced, too.[41]

Large paper envelopes are a little less high-tech, but do the job just as well. Put templates inside, information about the block on the outside. Don't forget the name of the block and a thumbnail sketch.[42]

Checking For Accuracy

Sew a sample block to make sure the templates have been accurately drawn and cut and to make sure the fabrics look well together. It could save hours of frustration later.

Chapter Notes

[1] Pat Morris: Glassboro, NJ.

[2] "How to Use the Patterns in Quilter's Newsletter," *Quilter's Newsletter Magazine,* #99 (February 1978) p. 27.

[3] Deanna Davis, in "Top Tip," *Quilter's Newsletter Magazine,* #201 (April 1988) p. 15.

[4] Chris DeTomasi: Lake Zurich, IL.

[5] Nancy Stucker: South Bend, IN.

[6] Kay Lukasko: Cinnaminson, NJ.

[7] Lois Smith: Rockville, MD.

[8] "100 Top Tips," *Quilter's Newsletter Magazine,* #100 (March 1978) p. 12.

[9] "Top Tips," *Quilter's Newsletter Magazine,* #164 (July/August 1984) p. 35.

[10] "Here's A Hint," *Quilter's Newsletter Magazine,* #208 (January 1989) p. 37.

[11] Mary Conroy: Sudbury, Ontario.

[12] Judy Martin, "Cutting Corners: Shortcut To Perfect Patchwork," *Quilter's Newsletter Magazine,* #173 (June 1985) p. 30-31.

[13] Jean V. Johnson: Olathe, KS.

[14] Judy B. Dales: Boonton Township, NJ.

[15] Ruth S. Kramer, in "Top Tips," *Quilter's Newsletter Magazine,* #20 (June 1971) p. 12.

[16] Sandi Fox: Los Angeles, CA. Shared by Nancy Dice: Bellevue, WA.

[17] Rosemary Koch: Arlington, MA.

[18] Jere Hansard, Supervisor, Diagnostic Radiology, Hurley Medical Center, Flint, MI.

[19] Claire Godin, in "Notes & Quotes," *Quilt World,* March/April 1981, p. 46.

[20] Ruth Spencer, in "Letters To The Editor," *Quilt World,* November/December 1980, p. 55.

[21] Irene Bartelt, in "Letter To The Editor," *Quilt World,* March/April 1981, p. 60.

[22] Mary Conroy: Sudbury, Ontario.

[23] May E. Bartlett: Brea, CA.

[24] Kay Nothiger, in "Notes & Quotes," *Quilt World,* September/October 1981, p. 16.

[25] Janis Klaus Gray: Springfield, IL.

[26]Iva Galloway, in "Top Tips," *Quilter's Newsletter Magazine*, #197 (November/December 1987) p. 70.

[27]Peggy M. Greene: Indianapolis, IN.

[28]Pat Morris, "The Mavericks In My Quilting Basket," *Quilt World*, May/June 1989, p. 8.

[29]Judy Anne Walter: Evanston, IL.

[30]Mrs. G. C. Spencer, in "Top Tip," *Quilter's Newsletter Magazine*, #210 (March 1989) p. 41.

[31]Naomi Jenks: Whitmore Lake, MI.

[32]Nancy Dice: Bellevue, WA.

[33]Linda Goodmon Emery: Derby, KS.

[34]Debra Radecky: Stow, OH.

[35]Erica S. Klahs, in "Top Tips," *Quilter's Newsletter Magazine*, #205 (September 1988) p. 53.

[36]Truly Knox, in "Top Tips," *Quilter's Newsletter Magazine*, #177 (November/December 1985) p. 55.

[37]Judy Anne Walter: Evanston, IL.

[38]"100 Top Tips," *Quilter's Newsletter Magazine*, #100 (March 1978) p. 14.

[39]Sharyn Craig: San Diego, CA.

[40]Catherine Anthony, as cited by Anita Murphy, "O Is For Organization," *Quilt Almanac*, 1984, p. 44.

[41]Mary Helen Wenz, in "Notes & Quotes," *Quilt World*, January/February 1980, p. 10.

[42]Mrs. Paul C. Olivia, in "Top Tips," *Quilter's Newsletter Magazine*, #25 (November 1971) p. 15.

CHAPTER FOUR
IRONING

Preparation

To clean a dirty iron, take a clean grocery sack and cut it open. Lay it on top of the ironing board and sprinkle it with table salt. Iron the salt.[1]

If the iron is in really bad shape, set it face down in a shallow baking pan or cookie sheet with sides. Add about 1/4" of white vinegar and allow the sole plate to soak for a few minutes. Wipe dry. For really stubborn stains (and an iron that is NOT coated with a non-stick surface) rub gently with steel wool.[2]

Soak the sole plate in vinegar for a good cleaning.

Silver polish will also clean the sole plate of your iron.[3] Rub the paste on with a damp sponge then rinse thoroughly. Use a cotton swab to remove excess polish from the steam holes.

If your home has hard water, it's best to fill your iron with distilled water.[4]

Iron over wax paper before each session and your iron will glide more smoothly.[5]

Ironing

When ironing fabric used for quilting, always do so with a light touch. And, just as importantly, move the iron over the fabric in the direction of the grain to minimize stretching and distortion. This is especially important when ironing near frayed edges.[6] The length of the goods is more able to absorb the motion of the iron than the cross-grain, which is more pliable and easier to stretch out of shape.[7]

To remove stubborn wrinkles, lay the piece to be ironed on a clean flat surface. Using a plant mister, mist it with warm water. Cover with the next piece of fabric to be ironed and mist that. Keep layering and misting, then flip the pile over and begin ironing with the first piece misted. To mist now and iron later, store the dampened fabric in a plastic bag.

If this seems like too much work, re-wet wrinkled fabric, put it through a spin cycle in the washing machine to remove most of the water, then pop it in the dryer. Take it out when it is still damp and iron immediately.[8]

Ironing Strategies

When ironing standard 44" wide fabric on a conventional ironing board, the pointed end tends to get in the way. To make things easier, and to increase the surface area slightly, turn the ironing board 180°, or stand on the other side of it. The fabric can simply hang off the square end.[9]

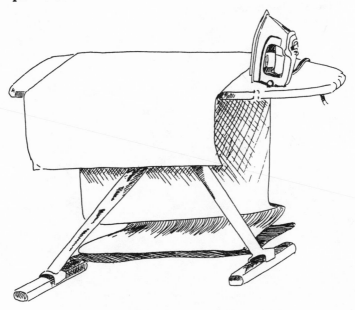

Iron on the "wrong" side of the board
for more surface area.

A very sharp pair of scissors can cut several layers of fabric at one time. Iron one fabric on top of another with a dry iron to build up "static cling." This will help to keep the layers from sliding when you cut.

Chapter Notes

[1]*The Ohio Valley Star*, as cited in "Some Nifty Ideas For Quilters," *Patchwork Patter*, August 1986, p. 13.

[2]Sharyn Craig: San Diego, CA.

[3]Julie Hussar: Linden, MI.

[4]Beebe Moss: Southfield, MI.

[5]Betty Bailey: East Alton, IL.

[6]Barbara Gunterman: Allen Park, MI.
[7]Jeffrey Gutcheon: New York.
[8]Peggy Greene: Indianapolis, IN.
[9]Rebecca C. Chaky: Moorepark, CA.

CHAPTER FIVE
MARKING

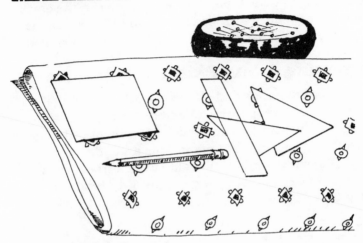

Finding Grainline

The easiest way to find the grain of a piece of cloth is to locate the selvage edge, that part of the cloth that is the most tightly woven. The grainline runs parallel to this edge.

If fabric has been cut and is missing the selvage, hold the fabric up to the light so that the weave of the fabric can be easily seen. Turn the fabric so that the threads are running horizontally and vertically, not diagonally. Place your fingers two to three inches apart and pull, first in one direction, then in the other. The straight of the goods, which runs parallel to the selvage edge, will stretch the least. The cross-grain, which runs perpendicular to the selvage edge, will stretch just slightly more. When fabric is pulled diagonally, with the bias, it will stretch the most.

Another way to locate the grainline is to position hands as indicated above and sharply tug at the fabric instead of gently pulling. Instead of seeing and feeling the difference, it is possible on most fabrics to *hear* the difference. Snapping the fabric with the grain will produce a high-pitched "pop," while snapping on the cross grain will produce a lower-pitched "thud." Take care to use the same force to snap the fabric in each direction.[1]

Creating A Non-Skid Work Surface

Fabric will slide and shift less during marking if a piece of fine sandpaper is placed under it. If no sandpaper is available, another piece of fabric placed underneath will keep things from moving around.[2]

To make a portable non-skid work surface, tuck a piece of fine sandpaper into a clipboard,[3] or glue it to a lap desk.[4]

Portable non-skid work surfaces.

Self-adhesive floor tiles can be outfitted with fine sandpaper for a handy surface on which to mark, too.[5]

If sandpaper isn't available, try placing fabric on top of a desk blotter. It is textured enough to hold the fabric in place, but won't wear down the point of the pencil.[6]

Marking Tools

A sliver of bath soap, without creams or oils, will mark dark fabrics nicely. Sharpen slivers in the shower by rubbing them until they are almost thin enough to see through. Allow them to dry before marking.[7]

"Non-photo" blue pencils, used to mark guide lines prior to offset printing, will leave a visible line on dark fabrics. Look for them in art and office supply stores.[8] Drafting pencils and artists' colored pencils can be used as well.

Keep pencils consistently sharp. Although fabric is a forgiving medium, thick lines in some places and thin lines in others don't make for accurate cutting or piecing.

For less drag on the fabric, angle pencils as close to the fabric as possible, and rest your index finger on top as you trace.[9]

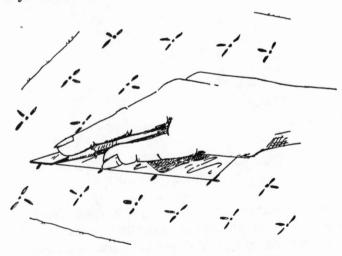

Angle pencils for less drag.

For the most accurate lines, hold the marking tool at the same angle on each side of the template.[10]

Mechanical pencils with thin, hard lead make dustless, narrow marks on light-colored fabric without ever having to be sharpened. Marks can also be lightened or removed with art gum or plastic erasers.[11]

Test every marking tool *before* using it to be sure it is completely removable. Test it on each piece of fabric you intend to use it on.

Marking Strategies

To differentiate between cutting lines and sewing lines when marking, use a solid line for sewing, and a dashed line for cutting.[12]

To mark cutting and sewing lines at the same time, use two standard hexagonal pencils rubber banded together.[13]

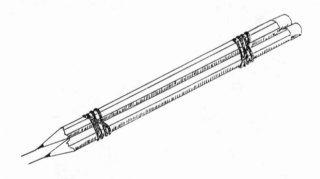

Use two pencils and a rubber band to mark
double lines 1/4" apart.

When making miniatures, use 1/2" seam allowance. "Fat" seam allowances make tiny pieces much easier to hang on to, and they can be trimmed down to a less bulky 1/8" after stitching.[14]

To avoid fabric waste, mark and cut borders and large pieces first, then mark and cut smaller pieces from the leftovers.[15]

Similarly, marking and cutting along the entire
length of the fabric first will also cut down on waste,
especially if there are other projects on the agenda
using the same cloth. The leftovers will be longer and
more versatile.[16]

Some solid fabrics have right and wrong sides just
as prints do. To tell one from the other, mark the wrong
side with random markings.[17]

To prevent unexpected color changes when joining
solid colors (some have not only a "right" and "wrong"
side, but also an "up" and a "down") and to keep track
of directional fabric, mark an arrow in the seam allowance of each patch immediately after tracing templates
to indicate which way the patch is to be sewn.[18]

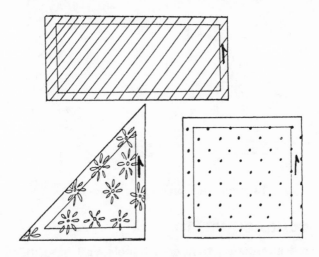

Mark patches with arrows to minimize confusion later.

With regularly patterned fabric or fabric printed
slightly off grain, ignore the grainline and line up the
edge of the template with the pattern printed on the fabric. Otherwise, a perfectly pieced block may have little
calico flowers marching off the edge of its patches![19]

Miters

Any right-triangle template can be used to mark miter lines on borders and bindings. Simply place the bottom even with the long side, and trace along the short side.[20]

Miter lines can also be created by folding. Just bring the short side parallel to the long side and press. The crease becomes the sewing line, from which a 1/4" seam allowance can be easily marked. Just open the fold and measure.

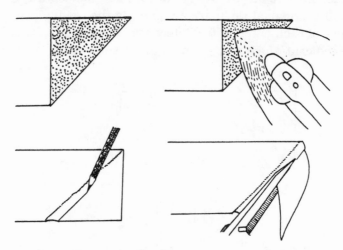

To miter: fold, press, mark, and cut.

Miscellaneous Tips

Have a tendency to misplace tools while marking? Try a carpenter's apron to keep track of rulers, marking tools, templates, scissors, rotary cutters, and other essentials.[21]

Fuse light-weight or slippery fabrics that stretch or fray uncontrollably, such as lamé, to iron-on interfacing. If the fabric is very sheer or so slippery that it won't hold a marked line, mark the interfacing.

Chapter Notes

[1] A student in a workshop in New Jersey showed me this tip. With her generosity, she planted the seed for this book.

[2] Phyllis Nye: Bonita Springs, FL.

[3] Mabel J. Hartley: Menasha, WI.

[4] Anita M. Barnard, in "Hints For Quilters," *Creative Quilting*, January/February 1989, p. 79.

[5] Carol Spaly: Ann Arbor, MI.

[6] Catherine Anthony: Houston, TX. Shared by Kay Lukasko: Cinnaminson, NJ.

[7] Judy Mathieson: Woodland Hills, CA.

[8] Debra Radecky: Stow, OH.

[9] Carol Potts: Chatham, IL.

[10] Pat Morris: Glassboro, NJ.

[11] Pat Morris, "Questions & Answers," *Quilt World*, January/February 1980, p. 28.

[12] Kay Lukasko: Cinnaminson, NJ.

[13] Julie Hussar: Linden, MI.

[14] Caroline Griffith: New Haven, CT. Shared by Pat Morris: Glassboro, NJ.

[15] Helen Squire, "Quilter's Queries," *Quilter's Newsletter Magazine,* #95 (October 1977) p. 11.

[16] Ellen B. Hess: Amlin, OH.

[17] "200 Top Tips," *Quilter's Newsletter Magazine*, #200 (March 1988) p. 11.

[18] Linda Goodmon Emery: Derby, KS.

[19] Pat Morris: Glassboro, NJ.

[20] Judy Anne Walter: Evanston, IL.

[21] Kay Burns, "Quilt-Words To The Quilt Wise: Ten Best Quilting Tips," *Quilt,* Spring 1989, p. 67.

CHAPTER SIX
CUTTING

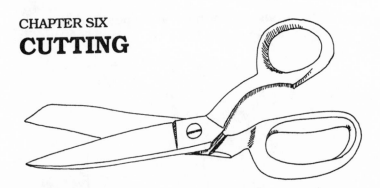

Scissors

Three pairs of scissors are better than one. Keep one pair for fabric, one for paper, and one for the rest of the family. Tag fabric scissors with yarn and a warning.

Intravenous (i.v.) tubing, tubing from fish tanks, and many other types of clear plastic tubing make excellent sheaths for small, sharp, pointy scissors.[1]

Use the right scissors for the job: Large shears for cutting patches, smaller ones for clipping curves and trimming stray threads.

Wiping scissor blades with fabric softening dryer sheets will help them glide through fabric more easily.[2]

To increase accuracy, cut patchwork pieces on a padded surface such as an ironing board, especially if several layers are cut at once. This will allow the scissors to sink a little below the fabric, causing less distortion. A hard surface will elevate the scissor blades, causing the layers of fabric to separate slightly and move out of alignment with the marked lines.[3]

For the sake of accuracy, cut just inside marked lines, as that most closely approximates the edge of the template.[4] When using right-handed scissors, cut clockwise; when using left-handed scissors (true left-handed scissors, where the blades are actually reversed), cut counter-clockwise. This will allow the top blade to move without obscuring the cutting line. To put it another way: hold the scrap and cut away the template.[5]

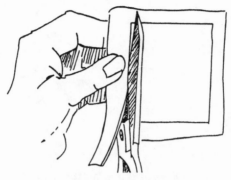

Cut just inside the marked line.

Instead of turning scissors to cut points and corners, cut each side all the way off, and then begin again at the next side.[6]

Cut background blocks for applique quilts 1/2" larger all the way around to compensate for any fraying that might occur while the block is handled. This will also allow for any "shrinkage" if there are many layers to be sewn. Once the applique is finished, blocks can be cut to the proper size and then assembled.[7]

Rotary Cutters

If your rotary cutter has lost its zip, even after a new blade has been put in, put a very small drop of sewing machine oil between the blade and the housing. Slice a few inches of scrap fabric to absorb any excess oil before cutting something important.[8]

To keep plexiglass rulers used with rotary cutters from slipping out of position, back them with non-skid stair treading, sold in hardware stores. It comes in various widths with a sandpaper-like finish on one side and self-adhesive on the other.[9]

Tape graph paper to the top and bottom of cutting mats for slicing widths in increments other than full inches. This is especially handy when cutting pieces for miniature quilts.[10]

Miscellaneous Tips

If you prefer to tear fabric instead of cutting it, clip off the corners immediately after tearing to reduce raveling. [11]

A paper cutter can cut up to two layers of fabric quickly, effortlessly and accurately. Use a weighted ruler to hold the edge securely.[12]

Chapter Notes

[1]Sally Pelikan: Wright City, MO.

[2]*El Paso Quilters' Association Newsletter*, February 1988, as cited in "Helpful Hints," *Trinity Valley Quilter's Guild Newsletter*, Vol. 6, No. 7 (March 1988) p. 9.

[3]Sharyn Craig: San Diego, CA.

[4]Margaret Umbenhower: Windsor, Ontario. Shared by Diana Boufford: Windsor, Ontario.

[5]Pat Morris: Glassboro, NJ.

[6]Ibid.

[7]Jeanne Emery: Grand Haven, MI.

[8]Sharyn Craig: San Diego, CA.

[9]Michael James: Somerset Village, MA.

[10]Becky Schaefer: Louisville, KY. From a 1988 Houston Quilt Festival participant.

[11]Holice Turnbow: Sheperdstown, WV.

[12]Jean Ray Laury: Clovis, CA.

CHAPTER SEVEN
HAND SEWING

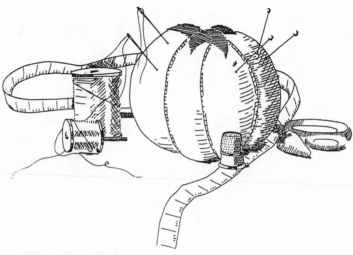

Work Surfaces

If neck and back muscles feel strained after sewing, try stitching with a bed pillow on your lap.[1] Raising the work is easier on the muscles than lowering your head.

Large ceiling tiles covered with a layer of batting or fleece and then with a layer of fabric make excellent lap tables upon which to piece or applique.[2]

Keeping Things Organized

Clip patches together with a spring action clothespin so they won't get mislaid.[3]

Another way to keep patches from getting lost is to stack them up, run a long thread through the stack, and wind the thread around the patches.

When storing or transporting work in progress, fold the raw edges towards the inside. If it is a large piece, fold it over a clothes hanger.[4]

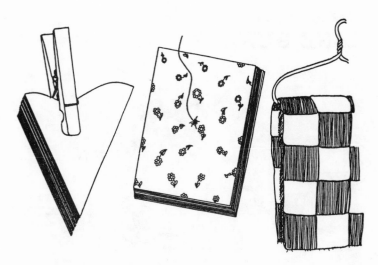

Keep patches organized.

Thread

Extra fine thread for lightweight fabric and machine embroidery is a good choice for hand applique as well. It is much finer and blends into the fabric better than regular hand sewing thread.[5]

To match thread to fabric lay the fabric out flat. Take every possible thread that might match and un-spool each about six inches. Lay the threads on the fabric running with the straight grain of the fabric and squint. The one you *don't* see is the one that matches best.[6]

If an applique project requires an assortment of different color threads, save space in your work basket by winding some of each color onto spare sewing machine bobbins.[7]

Threading Needles

The needle's eye is more clearly visible when the needle is held over a piece of white paper or cloth.[8]

To thread needles with very small eyes, hold the thread very tightly between your fingers and cut it at an angle with very sharp scissors. Then it will go right through.[9]

Stab at the eye of the needle with the thread in a downward motion for easier threading. [10]

If working with a needle threader is awkward and you need a "third" hand to hold the needle, stand the needle upright in a pincushion or work in progress, and then thread it.[11]

Sometimes needles thread more easily from one side than from the other. If the thread won't go in, turn the needle around and try from the other side. It couldn't hurt.[12]

Flatten wet thread before aiming it at the eye of the needle by pulling it between your tongue and front teeth or between two fingers. It will be easier to thread.

Still having trouble? Wet the back of the eye instead of wetting the thread. The moisture on the needle attracts the thread. Dry thread is also thinner and will go through the needle more easily.[13]

Avoiding Knots And Tangles

Sharply snapping a length of thread before cutting it off the spool will make it less likely to twist and knot.[14]

Running needle and thread through a fabric softening dryer sheet will keep the thread from knotting. Fold the dryer sheet into a little pillow and staple it together.[15] Rubbing fingers on the dryer sheet will also keep bits of thread from clinging to them.[16]

Waxing thread with a light coat of beeswax will keep it from fraying, twisting, and knotting. It will also make it slightly stiffer and easier to guide through the eye of the needle. Waxing transparent nylon thread is also beneficial.[17]

Out of beeswax? A white candle will work, too.[18]

An entire spool of thread can be waxed at one crack by submerging it in about 2" of melted paraffin. Melt the paraffin in an old pot or tin can on low heat. (Caution: It will burn if it gets too hot.) Lower the spool of thread into the paraffin and watch it bubble. When the bubbles stop (after about 20 minutes), remove the thread and place it on a piece of paper toweling to cool.[19]

Wax an entire spool at once.

Store the wax in its container in a plastic bag, dust free, until you need it again.[20] Excess wax can be removed by running a fingernail over the thread.[21]

Periodically stroking thread while sewing can help prevent tangles, too. Draw the needle all the way down the thread to the fabric. Then gently stroke the thread its entire length, from the fabric down to the end, to relax and unwind it.

Twisting thread can also be relaxed by dropping the threaded needle and allowing it to dangle and untwist itself.[22]

Rub polyester thread on a dry bar of soap to reduce static cling.[23]

To untangle looped knots (slip knots), pass the needle through the loop and pull up. Then put the needle under the knot and pull up until the knot is released.[24]

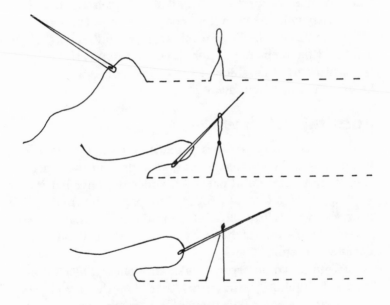

Untangle slip knots with your needle.

Needles And Pincushions

Running a needle through your hair seems to make the needle glide through the fabric more easily, either because of the static electricity produced or because of the thin coating of oil.[25]

The little strawberry dangling from the tomato-type pincushion is used for cleaning needles. Thrust needles and pins in and out to remove perspiration and tarnish.

A few pieces of felt sewn down the middle like a book is a safe place to store needles.[26]

Park needles and pins in the paper tops and bottoms of spools. Before discarding empty spools, shake them and listen for any needles or pins that might have been inadvertently pushed all the way through the paper. They can be retrieved by peeling off the paper.

Needles kept in cushions stuffed with human hair will stay sharper longer.[27] They'll also keep from rusting as they will receive a light coat of oil from the hair.[28]

A needle case made of wool fabric or quilted with wool batting keeps needles from rusting *forever!*[29]

Tear open pincushions to retrieve lost needles before throwing them away.[30]

Joining Patches

Position and re-position patches on a large sheet of freezer paper. When a satisfying arrangement is found, iron them in place and peel off the pieces as needed.[31]

Patches can also be arranged on paper that has been sprayed lightly with 3M Scotch™ Spray Mount® Artist's Adhesive. Patches stay in place, yet peel off easily for sewing.[32]

To cut down on errors, make and follow a block diagram when joining patches together.[33] Mark your place with Post-it™ notes. Lift them off and move them along as the work progresses. They won't leave a mark, and can be written on, too.[34]

To make a wrapped knot, commonly referred to as a "Quilter's Knot," hold the threaded needle between first finger and thumb and lay the end of the thread on the needle so that the cut end points toward the eye. Wrap the thread around the needle three times, more for a larger knot. Push the needle through the thread, and slide the knot to the end of the thread.[35]

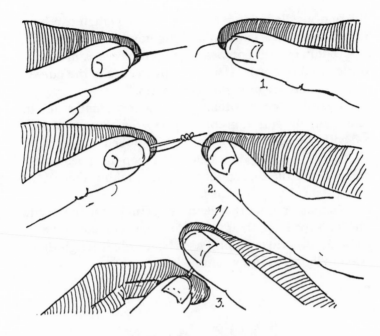

Making a wrapped knot.

If hitting knots from other seams with the needle is annoying when joining several patches together, try a "no knot" method. Begin each seam three or four stitches away from the end of the sewing line and sew towards the end. When you reach the end, turn and sew forward over the stitches you have just made, locking them in place. Seams can be ended in this way, too.

For greater ease in matching points, stitch each end first and then the middle. In other words, start at one corner and stitch towards the middle. Stop. Start again from the other corner and finish the seam in the middle.[36]

Pin one end of your work to your skirt or trouser leg for extra leverage and a "third hand." This is especially advantageous when joining small patches, as they won't be so hard to hang on to. By pulling gently with the non-needle holding hand, a running stitch can be taken much as it is when quilting in a hoop or frame.[37]

To join curved patches, clip both pieces at pre-designated intervals. Use the clips to ease in the curve and as reference or alignment points.[38]

To end a line of stitching, take a very small stitch in the seam allowance, grabbing just a few threads of fabric with the needle. As the needle is pulled, a loop of thread will appear. Just before the loop disappears, pass the needle through it and pull, making a small knot. Repeat several times.

To make a knot that is more secure, pass the needle through the loop, then watch for a second loop to be created from this action. Pass the needle through this second loop, too, for a double loop knot.[39]

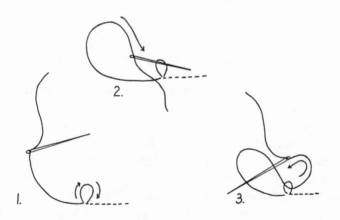

A double loop knot.

Miscellaneous Tips

Beginners attempting pictorial applique for the first time might find it helpful to transfer the pattern picture to a cotton voile base first and sew the pieces to the voile.[40]

Silk buttonhole twist is about the same thickness as three strands of embroidery floss and gives a beautiful sheen.[41]

When knotting embroidery floss (two or more strands), remove the needle and make several square knots at the surface of the fabric.[42]

Chapter Notes

[1]Lillian Holman, in "Top Tips," *Quilter's Newsletter Magazine*, #205 (September 1988) p. 53.

[2]Estelle Brown: Pasadena, MD.

[3]Pat Morris, "The Mavericks In My Sewing Basket," *Quilt World*, May/June 1980, p. 30.

[4]Ramona Wahl: Deer Lodge, MT. Shared by Lynda N.

Hammond: Deer Lodge, MT.

[5]Wanda Sieford: King Wood, TX. Shared by Judith Montano: Castle Rock, CO.

[6]Pat Morris: Glassboro, NJ.

[7]Pat Morris, "The Mavericks In My Quilting Basket," *Quilt World*, May/June 1980, p. 8.

[8]Grace Tanton, in "Top Tips," *Quilter's Newsletter Magazine*, #17 (March 1971) p. 10.

[9]Jinny Beyer: Great Falls, VA.

[10]Mabel J. Hartley: Menasha, WI.

[11]Sherry Sunday: New Kingstown, PA. Shared by Kay Lukasko: Cinnaminson, NJ.

[12]Pris DeVous: Dallas, TX.

[13]Shirley Fowlkes: Dallas, TX.

[14]Nancy Halpern: Natick, MA.

[15]Helen Kelley: Minneapolis, MN.

[16]Patricia Fullerton, in "Helps & Hints," *Craft Art Needlework Digest*, April 1988, p. 61.

[17]Doreen Leigh, in "Top Tips," *Quilter's Newsletter Magazine*, #209 (February 1989) p. 19.

[18]Helen W. Rose, "Pins, Needles, Thread And Knots For Patchwork," *Quilt World*, November/December 1981, p. 7.

[19]Ellen Camfield: Pittsford, NY. Shared by Jan Wass: Dawson, IL.

[20]Minnie Armstrong, in "Letter To The Editor," *Quilt World*, March/April 1982, p. 4.

[21]Ellen Camfield: Pittsford, NY, and Susan Kowalczyk: Utica, NY.

[22]Ramona Wahl: Deer Lodge, MT. Shared by Lynda N. Hammond: Deer Lodge, MT.

[23]Roxanna Fuhrman, in "Top Tips," *Quilter's Newsletter Magazine*, #209 (February 1989) p. 19.

[24]Clydia Wesley: Palestine, IL. Shared by Paul McDade: Hamilton, OH.

[25]Jo Diggs: Portland, ME.

[26]Sharyn Craig: San Diego, CA.

[27]Betty Kane, "For Small Hands: Quilters Gifts A Child Can Make," *Quilting USA*, Vol. 2, No. 2 (April 1988) p. 13.

[28]Barbara Nagy: St. Peters, MO.

[29]Carter Houck: New York.

[30]Marjorie Fetterhoff, *Quilter's Ranch Dispatch*, January/February 1987, p. 7.

[31]"200 Top Tips," *Quilter's Newsletter Magazine*, #200 (March 1988) p. 10.

[32]Carol Potts: Chatham, IL.

[33]Betsy Hatch, "There's Never Enough Time," *Quilt*, Spring 1986, p. 28.

[34]Patricia Fullerton, in "Helps & Hints," *Craft Art Needlework Digest*, April 1988, p. 61.

[35]Helen W. Rose, "Pins, Needles, Thread And Knots For Patchwork," *Quilt World*, November/December 1981, p. 7-8. Rose credits an unidentified student for teaching her.

[36]Donna Maki: Holt, MI.

[37]Creta M. Robinson: Ortonville, MI.

[38]Diana Boufford: Windsor, Ontario.

[39]Colleen K. Teichman: Kalispell, MT.

[40]Carole K. McMichael: Hewitt, TX.

[41]Judith Montano: Castle Rock, CO.

[42]Cecilia Phillips: Northport, AL.

CHAPTER EIGHT
MACHINE SEWING

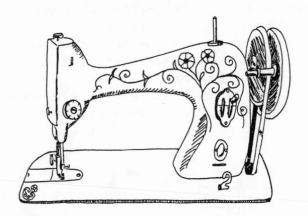

Getting Ready

Few things are more frustrating than trying to stitch with a sewing machine that is not in good working order. Be sure to follow manufacturer's recommendations on cleaning, oiling, and routine maintenance. Learn how your machine works and how to keep it in good shape.

Each time the bobbin is changed, take a swipe at the dust behind the bobbin case with a cleaning brush. What the brush can't reach, a can of compressed air might be able to dislodge. If it doesn't fly right out, take a cotton swab to remove loosened dirt and dust.[1]

A feather will also help you reach and clean those hard-to-get-at places inside your sewing machine. It is easy to manipulate and surprisingly resilient.[2]

To keep the foot pedal on your sewing machine from wandering away as you sew, try placing more of your foot on it. The weight of your heel resting on the pedal (instead of on the floor) is less likely to push the pedal away each time it is depressed.[3]

A piece of rubber-backed carpeting will keep your foot pedal corralled on a wood or linoleum floor.[4] Place another piece of carpeting under the sewing machine to deaden the sound and to keep the machine from walking off the table on high-speed seams.

For something more secure on carpeted floors, press a piece of self-adhesive Velcro® (hook side) to the underside of the foot control.[5]

If it's difficult to get a good grip on the hand wheel to move the needle up and down, wrap a few wide rubber bands around it for added traction.

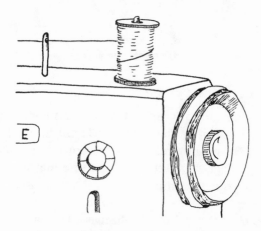

Rubber bands around the hand wheel provide traction.

Needles, Thread, And Pins

Sewing machine needles come in different sizes and should be matched to the thread and fabric being used. Check specifications in your sewing machine manual or with the dealer or fabric shop.

Small burrs on sewing machine needles can be smoothed by stroking them across a sharpening stone. Turn the needle as you move it back and forth, rejuvenating the point.

Before beginning any major project, wind several bobbins with the thread you need. That way, when one is used up, time won't be wasted refilling it.[6]

If you can't force yourself to do that for fear of winding up with a half dozen *leftover* spools of chartreuse, wind all your bobbins with natural colored sewing thread or a neutral dark, and use them for everything.[7]

Many machines can wind extra bobbins while they sew. This makes winding bobbins almost painless.[8]

To prevent thread from winding around the spindle, make sure spools are placed on the sewing machine with the little cut that anchors the thread on *top*.[9]

Or tape a tapestry needle alongside the spool, and pass the thread through the eye before threading the rest of the machine.[10]

Magnetic pincushions not only catch pins tossed in their general direction, they can also be passed over stray pins hastily "flipped" out during frantic sewing sessions. Handy as they are, however, remember to keep them away from computerized sewing machines as they can foul up the machine's memory.[11]

Make your own pin catcher out of self-adhesive magnetic tape, found in discount and craft supply stores. Cut to the length desired, peel off the backing, and stick it on wood, metal, or fabric.[12]

Measuring Standard Seam Allowance

Many sewing machines have a built-in 1/4" measure for sewing standard patchwork seam allowances: the edge of the presser foot. The distance from the right side of the presser foot to the needle in its center position measures 1/4". If this is not the case with your machine, take a ruler, locate 1/4" from the needle, and mark it on the throat plate with a piece of masking tape.[13] Run the masking tape over the entire width of the throat plate for the most accurate piecing.[14]

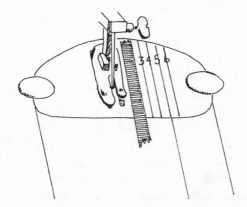

Masking tape marks 1/4" from the needle.

The masking tape can also be layered by adding one strip on top of another until a little ridge is formed. This will keep the fabric from accidently sliding over the mark.

If you find the ruler sliding around before you are able to place the tape, slip a piece of 1/4" graph paper under the presser foot. When the needle is lowered through one line, the 1/4" mark you're after is the very next line to the right.[15]

A strip of Dr. Scholl's® molefoam® placed 1/4" from the needle will also guide patchwork along a raised edge. It has a peel-and-stick backing which leaves no sticky residue so it can be moved for wider or narrower seam allowances at will.[16]

Hard plastic tape used in label-making machines will also give a raised edge to follow.[17]

If sticking something to your sewing machine offends your sensibilities, a simple line can be drawn on the machine with a fine point permanent marker.[18]

Sitting *directly* in front of the needle will help you guide the fabric through the machine more easily, whichever seam allowance guide you choose to follow.[19]

Machine Piecing Strategies

When sewing fabric strips together whose finished width will be 1/4" (Seminole work, string piecing, etc.), line up the left-hand edge of the presser foot with the previous seam line and sew. Obviously, this only works if the presser foot is an accurate 1/4" measure. If it isn't, try one of the tips mentioned above to mark the left-hand side and sew.[20]

You can save time, thread, and energy by "chain piecing." Without lifting the presser foot, feed the patches to be joined through the machine one pair right after the other. Leave just enough room (between 1/8" and 1/4") separating each unit so that they can be easily clipped apart later.[21]

"Chain piecing" is fast and easy.

The only time-waster comes right at the beginning when the threads must be held back behind the presser foot as the chain starts. This can be eliminated by doing it only once. After the last unit is sewn, slip in a 2" x 2" scrap of fabric, folded in half, and sew into it. Clip the threads to release the patchwork, but leave the

2" x 2" piece of fabric in the machine. Next time another string of patches is ready to go through the machine, there will be no loose threads to monkey with. You won't even have to lift the presser foot![22]

When working with long bias seams, draw the template shape on the fabric, then stay-stitch between the cutting and sewing lines before cutting the shape out of fabric.[23]

Matching Points

Alternating the direction in which seam allowances are pressed helps get points to meet precisely, by making it easy to butt seams together.[24]

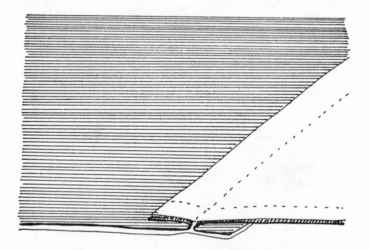

Butt seam allowances to match points.

For really tough seams, machine baste patches together before joining them with a regular machine stitch. Take it out of the machine and open the patches. If they don't match, it will be much easier to rip. If they do, just sew over the basting with a tighter stitch.[25]

Many sewing machines feed the fabric unevenly. Usually the bottom is pushed along faster than the top. To compensate, take special care to pin seams and guide them through deliberately. To take advantage, put bias pieces and patches that are a little too big on the bottom and let the uneven feed take up the slack. If patches are way off but still salvageable, put them on the bottom and ease them in by stretching the seam as you sew.

There is a built-in guide to follow when piecing triangles. After one triangle has been sewn to another and has been laid on top of the next piece or unit, look for the "X," or the intersection of the two previous seams. It should be 1/4" from the top edge. If the pieces have been pressed well, it should be easy to sew right through the "X" and get a perfect point. [26]

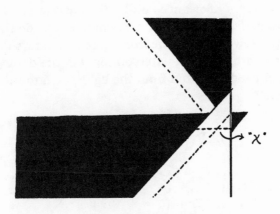

X marks the spot.

If slippery fabrics are driving you crazy, slip a piece of wax paper between them and sew. The wax paper will hold them together and can be torn away after the seam is sewn.[27]

Pressing

Cotton ironing board covers are better than shiny Teflon™ ones as they reflect less heat.[28]

Cover a small table or stool with a heavy towel and keep it near the sewing machine. Seams can then be pressed immediately, without getting up.[29]

A small piece of plywood padded with flannel and covered in a bright print is a perfect portable ironing board that can be moved around the room at will.[30]

The cardboard inside a bolt of fabric, wrapped first in needlepunched batting, and then in fabric, makes a soft, lightweight portable ironing board. Loose ends can be tucked in, taped, pinned, or basted.[31]

The most portable ironing surface is a folded bed sheet. Keep folding until it becomes a manageable size and is thick enough to protect the surface upon which it is placed.[32]

Press seam allowances under the darkest patch to make them less noticeable.[33] A simple way to do this is to lay the sewn unit on the ironing board, right sides together, with the dark patch on top. Lift the dark patch and slide the iron from the light patch to the dark patch.

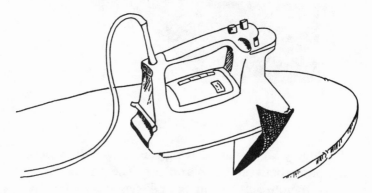

Press seams to the darker side.

Press blocks with many pieces over a thick towel using your steam iron.[34] Dampen the towel and your job will be easier.

Use an iron to straighten and block patchwork. To make this easier, draw perfect squares directly on your ironing board cover with a permanent pen.[35]

Machine Applique

To turn corners when satin stitching, leave the needle down and pivot. To make sure the bobbin thread has been caught, use the hand wheel to start the needle on its way up before pivoting. Lift the presser foot only partially, just enough to let the fabric turn, so tension on the upper thread will be maintained.[36]

Save fabric softener sheets to stabilize applique. Place them under backgrounds and sew. After the applique is stitched, they can be torn away.[37]

Miscellaneous Tips

For straight seams less than six inches long, don't bother pinning. Place right sides together with raw edges even and *iron* them together. Then sew.[38]

Tape a paper lunch sack to the edge of the sewing machine table to catch stray threads and small fabric pieces. Sure beats trying to hit a wastepaper basket on the other side of the room.[39]

Make a clean job of ripping with masking tape. Using a seam ripper, slice every third stitch or so, then cover the "ripped" seam with masking tape. Flip the patch over and pull the long thread out. Flip a second time to remove the tape and all the little threads now stuck to it![40]

Chapter Notes

[1]Sharyn Craig: San Diego, CA.

[2]Anita Murphy: Kountze, TX.

[3]Beebe Moss: Southfield, MI.

[4]Anita Murphy: Kountze, TX.

[5]"200 Top Tips," *Quilter's Newsletter Magazine*, #200 (March 1988) p. 10.

[6]"100 Top Tips," *Quilter's Newsletter Magazine*, #100 (March 1978) p. 12.

[7]Sharyn Craig: San Diego, CA.

[8]Holice Turnbow: Sheperdstown, WV.

[9]Phyllis Colliver: Clio, MI.

[10]Robbie and Tony Fanning, *The Complete Book Of Machine Quilting* (Radnor, PA: Chilton Book Company, 1980) p. 45.

[11]Louise Patterson, in "Tips And Brilliant Ideas," *Canada Quilts*, Vol. XVII, No. 5 (November 1988) p. 28.

[12]"Quilter's Tip," *Portage Patchwords*, Vol. 2 (Summer 1987) p. 4.

[13]"100 Top Tips," *Quilter's Newsletter Magazine*, #100 (March 1978) p. 14.

[14]Helen Kelley: Minneapolis, MN.

[15]Barbara Caron: Falcon Heights, MN.

[16]Sharyn Craig: San Diego, CA. Sharyn learned this from a teacher of the blind.

[17]Judy Mathieson: Woodland Hills, CA. Judy learned this from a student in North Carolina.

[18]Betsy Hatch: Arcadia, CA.

[19]Judy Anne Walter: Evanston, IL.

[20]Sharyn Craig: San Diego, CA.

[21]Marsha McCloskey, *Wall Quilts* (Bothell, WA: That Patchwork Place, 1983) p. 11-12.

[22]Jan Myers-Newbury: Pittsburgh, PA.

[23]Nancy Halpern: Natick, MA.

[24]Betsy Hatch, "There's Never Enough Time!" *Quilt*, Spring 1986, p. 28.

[25]Gay Imbach, as cited by Betsy Hatch, "There's Never Enough Time!" *Quilt*, Spring 1986, p. 28.

[26]Betsy Hatch: Arcadia, CA.

[27]"200 Top Tips," *Quilter's Newsletter Magazine*, #200 (March 1988) p. 11.

[28]Pat Morris: Glassboro, NJ.

[29]Kay Burns, "Quilt-Words To The Quilt Wise: Ten Best Quilting Tips," *Quilt*, Spring 1989, p. 67.

[30]Jean Ray Laury: Clovis, CA.

[31]Sharyn Craig: San Diego, CA.

[32]Kay Lukasko: Cinnaminson, NJ.

[33]"100 Top Tips," *Quilter's Newsletter Magazine*, #100 (March 1978) p. 11.

[34]Edith Soltis, in "Top Tips," *Quilter's Newsletter Magazine*, #61 (November 1974) p. 17.

[35]"100 Top Tips," *Quilter's Newsletter Magazine*, #100 (March 1978) p. 12.

[36]Linda Halpin, "Steps To Better Machine Applique," *Quilting Today*, #9 (October/November 1988) p. 49.

[37]Julie Hussar: Linden, MI.

[38]Barbara L. Crane: Lexington, MA.

[39]Beebe Moss: Southfield, MI.

[40]Robbie and Tony Fanning, *The Complete Book Of Machine Quilting* (Radnor, PA: Chilton Book Company, 1980) p. 94.

CHAPTER NINE
MARKING THE QUILT TOP

Drafting The Design

Inexpensive shelf paper, without wax or adhesive, works great for drafting quilting designs for large blocks and borders.[1]

If plain paper is hard to find, try the paper with which physicians cover their examination tables. It can be purchased most economically in 225 foot rolls, and in varying widths, at most medical supply stores. It's thin enough to see a line through and is surprisingly resilient.

Commercial templates and stencils can be enlarged or reduced on a copy machine. Trace them on paper first, then size them up or down.

To transfer a quilting design from quilt to paper, lay the quilt on a bed over a piece of tissue paper. Carefully push a long thin pin through the quilt and into the tissue paper along the quilting lines. Or, place a large plastic dry cleaner's bag over the quilt, and carefully follow the quilting design with a felt tip pen.[2]

If the plastic bag makes you nervous, large sheets of acetate can be purchased at art supply stores and placed over quilts to "lift" the quilting patterns.[3]

Once the pattern is on paper it can be slid under light-colored fabric and traced fairly easily. If the pattern is difficult to see, place a piece of white paper under the paper pattern, or use a light box.[4]

If the paper pattern slips, coat it with a thin layer of 3M Scotch™ Spray Mount® Artist's Adhesive before placing the fabric on top.[5]

Paper patterns can also be covered with Con-tact® paper to keep ink from smearing and to strengthen the paper for repeated use.[6]

Light Boxes

The best way to transfer quilting designs from paper to fabric is with a light box. Commercial light boxes are expensive, but with a little ingenuity you can make your own.

There may already be a light box in your dining room. Any table with leaves will work. Pull the table apart and replace one leaf with a piece of plexiglass or a storm window. Move a table lamp or flashlight under the table. Lay the paper pattern on top, then the quilt top, and start tracing.[7] Glass top coffee tables are instant light boxes. Just add the light.

Have a top-loading washer? Open the lid, throw in a flashlight, and pop a storm window on top. If the washing machine comes with its own light, forget the flashlight. Want to use the flashlight? Stick it inside a trash can and put the storm window on top. If nothing else it will force you to wash at least one storm window, not to mention the trash can.

Taping paper patterns and fabric to a window will work, but only with small projects, and only during daylight hours.

If you enjoy working on a vertical surface, tape everything to the television set. Turn it on, turn the volume down, and tune it to a station it doesn't get.[8]

Old hard-sided suitcases[9] and wooden soda pop cases[10] can be outfitted with light bulbs and plexiglass, too.

Other Transferring Techniques

To transfer designs from books and magazines, lay a piece of netting over the design and trace with a permanent marker. Then position the netting on top of the fabric, pin it in place, and trace the design through the netting.[11]

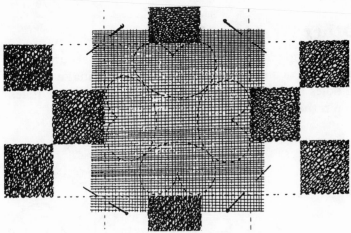

Trace patterns with netting.

Quilting designs can also be taken to the print shop and copied, or traced onto carbon paper. Then iron the designs onto the fabric. Test to make sure that the copier ink or carbon paper you choose will wash out.[12]

Dressmaker's carbon (yellow is preferred) can be used to transfer quilting designs. Slide the carbon under the design and over the fabric to be marked. Use a dressmaker's wheel or a blunt pencil to trace the design. Test first to make sure it will wash out.[13]

A fat crochet hook will also give good results without damaging the original.[14]

Use a "pounce" to transfer patterns. First draw the design on cardboard and perforate it every 1/4" or so with a darning needle. Turn the cardboard over and run the needle through the holes from the back side, too. Place it on the fabric, load a piece of batting with corn starch, and press the corn starch through the template. Connect the dots with a longer lasting marking tool, and blow away the corn starch.[15] Perforations can also be made on the sewing machine, just remove the thread.[16]

Other Marking Methods

To keep plastic or cardboard templates secure while tracing, use a small-holed paper punch to make pairs of holes in the template about 3/8" apart. Use the holes to pin the template to the fabric.[17]

Pin templates in place.

Mark quilting designs with a large, dull tapestry needle over a hard surface. The resulting indentation shows up well on dark fabrics and has no chemicals that might harm the fabric in years to come.[18] If the marks are hard to see, adjust the angle of the light.[19]

A slick way to mark cross-hatching lines is to use eight-to-the-inch Bargello canvas. Mark your lines on the canvas exactly where you want them, place it over the fabric, and run a pencil down each line. The resulting dashed lines are straight, easy to follow, and can also serve as a guide to evenly spaced quilting stitches.[20]

Mark As You Go

If you like to quilt the standard 1/4" from all seam lines, can't "eyeball" the distance with any accuracy, and aren't crazy about marking every quilting line, try 1/4" masking tape. Just stick it on the quilt so that one edge touches the seam line, and quilt along the other side. Avoid nicking the edge of the tape with the needle, as this can really gum up the works, and never leave the tape on the quilt for very long, especially in warm weather.

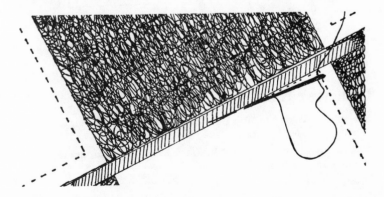

Use masking tape for a consistent 1/4" guide.

Is masking tape fun? Try Chartpak® tape. It's used for drafting and comes in a variety of widths ranging from 1/64" to 1".[21]

Cut quilting stencils out of Con-tact® paper. Stick them in place and quilt around them.[22]

Miscellaneous Tips

Freeze soap slivers and use them to mark quilting designs on dark fabrics.[23]

Faded marks from water-soluble marking pens can be seen anew under a black light and re-marked.[24]

Find faded marks under a black light.

Chapter Notes

[1]Martha B. Skelton, in "Top Tips," *Quilter's Newsletter Magazine,* #33 (July 1972) p. 10.

[2]Gladys Cooper, in "Top Tips," *Quilter's Newsletter Magazine,* #168 (January 1985) p. 47.

[3]Diana Smicklevich: Ravenna, OH.

[4]Linda Halpin, "Applique Elegance-Part 4," *Quilting Today,* #9 (October/November 1988) p. 40-41.

[5]Carol Potts: Chatham, IL.

[6]Myrtle E. Stone, in "Top Tips," *Quilter's Newsletter Magazine,* #83
(September 1976) p. 27.

[7]Judy Anne Walter: Evanston, IL.

[8]Linda Halpin, "Applique Elegance-Part 4," *Quilting Today,* #9
(October/November 1988) p. 41.

[9]Sara Carr: Charlotte, NC.

[10]Betsy Freeman: Sanibel, FL. Shared by Pauline Wetterstroem: Le-
high Acres, FL.

[11]Karen Tolliver: Ashland, KY.

[12]Pat Flynn Kyser, "Pieces & Patches," *Quilt World,* July/August
1982, p.7.

[13]Debra Radecky: Stow, OH.

[14]Betty Chism, in "Top Tips," *Quilter's Newsletter Magazine,* #170
(March 1985) p. 47.

[15]Mary Conroy: Sudbury, Ontario.

[16]"100 Top Tips," *Quilter's Newsletter Magazine,* #100 (March
1978) p. 12.

[17]Lois K. Ide: Bucyrus, OH.

[18]Sandi Fox: Los Angeles, CA. Shared by Nancy Dice: Bellevue, WA.

[19]Nancy Dice: Bellevue, WA.

[20]Pat Coventry, as cited in "Helpful Hints From Indiana Quilters,"
Lady's Circle Patchwork Quilts, February/March 1987, p. 62.

[21]Betsy Hatch, "Tools And Gadgets," *Quilt Almanac,* 1987, p. 73.

[22]"200 Top Tips," *Quilter's Newsletter Magazine,* #200 (March
1988) p. 10.

[23]Elly Sienkiewicz, in "Top Tips," *Quilter's Newsletter Magazine,*
#203 (June 1988) p. 48.

[24]Suzanne Gainer, in "Top Tips," *Quilter's Newsletter Magazine,*
#199 (February 1988) p. 46.

CHAPTER TEN

STRETCHING AND BASTING

Preparing The Top And Lining

To keep quilt tops from stretching out of shape, especially on bias edges, machine stitch around the edges.

Binding can be sewn onto the top before basting. This will prevent edges from raveling.[1]

If a heat sensitive marking tool has not been used, give the top one last pressing to make sure seams are straight and seam allowances are under the appropriate patches. Be sure to clip all stray threads.

Baste seams that won't stay in the right place, remembering to put knots on the right side so they can be removed painlessly after quilting. This is especially handy when trying to keep seam allowances in the lining all running in the same direction.[2]

For perfect seams on the quilt lining, first press them closed to set the thread into the fabric. Then press them open for sharp, straight creases without puckers. Finally, press them to one side to keep batting from oozing out.[3]

Save time and energy by basting and quilting on the same frame. A simple old-fashioned frame of 1 x 2s and C-clamps is something you can make yourself. To find the length of each board, measure each side of the quilt, and add 4" for the lining and another 4" for the overlap of the boards. Tack a strip of fabric to each board so that it hangs over a couple of inches, and prop the whole thing up on chairs, TV trays, or other stray pieces of furniture. After the quilt is basted, the two long side boards can be replaced with two shorter ones and the quilt rolled to a more manageable size.

Batting

Unfold batting and let it "rest" overnight before basting. It will be less wrinkled and easier to handle in the morning.

Bonded batts of high quality can be put in the dryer at the lowest setting for five to 10 minutes to fluff.[4] They can also be tumbled with a damp washcloth, if desired.[5]

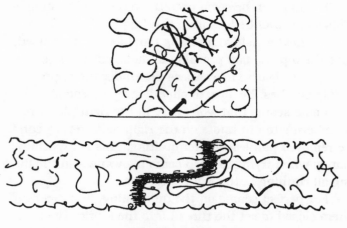

Butt batting, then stitch.

If the batting is too small, it can be spliced. Carefully split the batting in half along the edges to be joined. Try not to split more than about 1" deep. Peel back the top layers and cut off a strip about 1/2" wide on each piece. Flip one piece over, butt them together, and baste with a herringbone stitch.

Cotton batting can be spliced by first tearing each edge and then laying one torn edge on top of the other. They'll stick together seamlessly and will stay together by the close quilting required on natural fiber batts.[6]

Stretching

Mark the middle of each side of the quilt top, the lining, and the stretching boards. Use the marks as placement guides.

A piece of string anchored with thumb tacks and tightly stretched from one side of the frame to the other can help line up blocks vertically and horizontally before they are basted in place.[7]

Measure the distance between the edge of the lining and the edge of the board as each side is pinned to make sure fabric is stretched consistently. Do this for the quilt top as well.

Mist the lining, batting, and top during the stretching process to help relax the fabric, flatten problem areas, and "block" the quilt.[8]

Basting

There seem to be two schools of thought regarding basting. One suggests basting from the center out, the other from one side to the other in a grid pattern. Both recommend basting thoroughly.

Instead of cutting lengths of basting thread, let the action of the needle pull it off the spool as each stitch is taken. Cut the thread after several feet have been basted, hopefully before it breaks on its own. It should tangle less this way and will be easier to pull out later. This technique is especially handy if friends have been invited to a "baste off." Line them up on either side of the quilt with a spool and threaded needle. The first one starts basting and, when she can't reach any farther, passes the needle to the next one in line. She sews, passes the needle to the next one, and so on. Meanwhile the first one threads up another spool and begins the next row![9]

Baste with an embroidery or a crewel needle into a spoon. Place the quilt on a hard surface and use the bowl of the spoon to push the quilt just in front of the needle down and out of the way. As the point of the needle hits the spoon it will glide up the bowl of the spoon where it can be easily gripped and pulled through.[10]

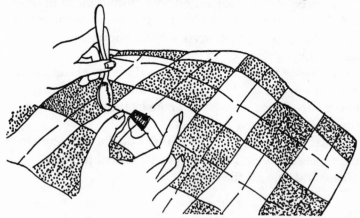

Baste on a hard surface into a spoon.

If thread basting is tedious, try pin basting with small rust-proof brass safety pins. They should be put in parallel to the frame boards that will be rolled, so as not to tear the quilt. When quilting in a hoop, take care not to get them caught as the top part of the hoop is put in place.

Chapter Notes

[1]Jill Le Croissette: Carlsbad, CA.

[2]Edna Dombroske: Midland, MI.

[3]Nancy Jacoby: Wabash, IN.

[4]H.D. Wilbanks, as cited by Mary Reddick, "The Batting Story," *Quilter's Newsletter Magazine*, #180 (March 1986) p. 35.

[5]Jo Grimes: Ft. Worth, TX.

[6]Judy Anne Walter: Evanston, IL.

[7]Bea Walroth, in "Tips And Brilliant Ideas," *Canada Quilts*, Vol. XVII, No. 5 (November 1988) p. 28.

[8]Barbara Caron: Falcon Heights, MN.

[9]Judy Anne Walter: Evanston, IL.

[10]Pat Morris: Glassboro, NJ.

CHAPTER ELEVEN
THIMBLES

What To Look For

Few things can improve your quilting stitch like a good thimble. Look for one with wide deep dimples on the top. If deep dimples are nowhere to be found, look for one with a raised lip.

If your thimble is "dimple-less," it may still be able to catch a needle until you can find a better one. Make a dent in the top with the head of a roofing nail. A few taps with a rolling pin should do it.[1]

Homemade leather thimbles can be made from two finger tips cut off a pair of old leather gloves. Tuck the smaller one inside the larger one and start sewing.[2]

Sizing

If a thimble is too big, coat the inside with several layers of nail polish. Or wrap a few pieces of masking tape around the inside and dust with corn starch or talcum powder to lessen the sticky feeling.

Make a too-big thimble oval instead of round by tapping it lightly on the side with a hammer. It might fit better.[3]

Keep an assortment of slightly different size thimbles handy to accommodate seasonal changes in finger size.[4]

Slipping

Blow into the thimble to keep it from occasionally falling off your finger.

Licking your finger will accomplish the same thing.[5]

A small piece of Dr. Scholl's® molefoam® on the inside of a thimble will keep it snug.[6]

Glue stick on the tip of your finger will keep a leather thimble from moving around.[7]

Miscellaneous Tips

Because most quilters seem to hit the same spot on their thimbles over and over again, usually without realizing it, it's a good idea not to put thimbles on the same way each time. Use decorative marks, engraved initials, or other distinguishing marks to indicate which way you're putting it on. Also, try to guide the needle with a different part of the thimble's surface to avoid wearing one particular spot too thin, especially if you're using a silver thimble.

If you suspect a hole, hold the thimble up to the light before putting it on to find the hole before the needle does.

To prevent thimbles from rusting and staining fingers, coat them with a thin layer of nail polish. If fingers should become stained, lemon juice will remove the discoloration.

Chapter Notes

[1] Gail Chatterson: Howell, MI.

[2] "200 Top Tips," *Quilter's Newsletter Magazine*, #200 (March 1988) p. 10.

[3] Jane Bosch, in "Top Tips," *Quilter's Newsletter Magazine*, #183 (June 1986) p. 41.

[4] Cathy Grafton: Pontiac, IL.

[5] Nancy Dice: Bellevue, WA.

[6] "200 Top Tips," *Quilter's Newsletter Magazine*, #200 (March 1988) p. 10.

[7] Jeannette T. Muir, in "Top Tip," *Quilter's Newsletter Magazine*, #193 (June 1987) p. 54.

CHAPTER TWELVE

QUILTING

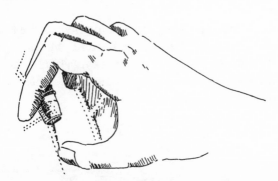

Strategies For Hoops And Frames

Hoops without pedestals can be propped up on the edge of a TV tray.[1]

To quilt corners and edges using a hoop, baste the edges to a towel. One which closely approximates the thickness of the quilt is best. Put the towel between the two hoops and sew.[2]

To keep sewing tools from rolling off the hoop each time it is jostled or set down, load the quilt into the hoop upside-down. Place the larger hoop against the lining, and the smaller hoop against the top.[3]

Reversing the hoops.

For tools always at arm's length, run a length of yarn through the screw at the top of the hoop. Tie a pair of scissors at one end and a spool of thread at the other.[4]

Eight long shoe laces, four tied to the top part of the hoop and four tied to the bottom, will help you roll and tie a bulky quilt out of the way. When tying the laces, tie them as close to the ends as possible for the longest tails.[5]

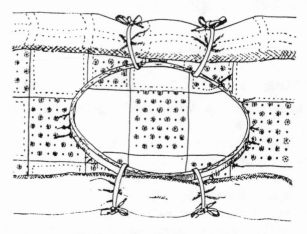

Tie the quilt out of your way.

For quilters who enjoy working on a frame, there's nothing like a secretarial chair that swivels for reaching hard-to-quilt places. Get one with an air lift for comfortable sitting at any height.

If everything about a frame sounds appealing save for the space it takes up, sink four large hooks into your ceiling. When you're finished quilting for the day, hoist it up![6]

When many people gather to quilt around the frame, plan to have a "reader." It's the perfect job for someone who can no longer quilt but still wants to get involved.[7]

For those quilting alone, "Talking Books" from the local library are the answer.[8]

When the quilting session is over, cover the frame with a folding cardboard cutting board to protect work from sunlight and the cat.[9]

An old sheet[10] (or a length of muslin) folded in two placed over the frame will shield the quilt from dirt and sunlight.

Needles And Thread

Most agree: The smaller the needle, the smaller the stitch. If quilting with small needles is awkward, hand piece with them first. After an entire quilt top with a between, it will feel like an old friend.[11]

Since platinum needles look just like needles made of nickle plated steel, park them on a small piece of high contrast fabric glued to the side of your pincushion.[12]

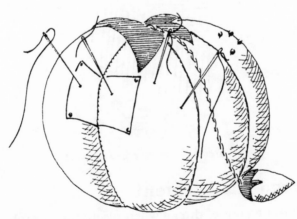

A special place for special needles.

If it's hard to find short quilting needles in the pincushion, leave them threaded with a short length of bright thread.[13]

If a needle handles unpredictably, it might be bent. A quick glance will tell if it's a real boomerang. To tell if it's only slightly out of kilter, roll it between your first finger and thumb and see if it wobbles.

Since threading needles in mid-stream takes too much time, thread more than one needle before beginning. How about an entire pack? Two packs?[14]

Not sure how long each thread should be ahead of time? Thread an entire pack of needles onto *one* spool of thread. Pull the thread and the first needle to the desired length while holding the others back. Tuck the thread in the cut at the top of the spool, then clip the thread.[15]

Thread all the needles at once.

Thread Management

Running out of thread when piecing is no problem; running out with just half an inch to go when quilting is infuriating. To put off the inevitable for just a few more stitches, pierce the tail of the thread about 1/2" from the end with the point of the needle. (It sometimes helps to place the thread on the edge of the hoop or

frame to stabilize it.) Pull the thread over the rest of the
needle, making a slip knot at the eye, and continue
sewing.[16] This is also a great way to teach kids to sew.
The needle can't un-thread itself.

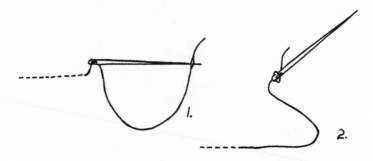

Split the tail to "make" more thread.

If chasing spools of quilting thread across the floor
isn't your idea of fun, capture them in an empty half
pound margarine tub, with a small hole cut in the lid.
Pull the thread through the hole as needed, free from
twists and tangles. Other sewing tools will fit in it as
well.[17]

Smaller tubs, just for the thread, are handy, too. If
the thread slides down the hole and back into the tub,
add two more holes and pass the end through.

Extra large prescription bottles can corral spools of
quilting thread with one slight modification. Melt a
small hole in the side with a hot ice pick. Then pop the
thread in, thread the end through, and snap on the
lid.[18]

To keep new spools of quilting thread from unwinding uncontrollably, un-spool about 6" of thread. Wrap
the thread around the spool once, catching a finger underneath. Then thread the end under the loop made by
the finger, creating a slip knot. You can pull the thread
off the spool, but it will never unwind on its own.

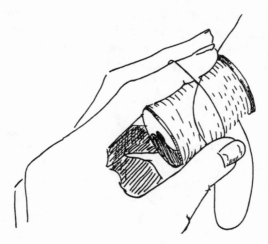

A slip knot keeps the thread from unwinding.

Grabbing Needles

Keep a small pair of pliers nearby to pull out over-loaded needles.[19] Pieces of old dead balloons, finger cots from the local medical supply house, and the rubber finger shields postal workers and secretaries wear also work.

Since the rubber finger shields are fairly stiff, they can be sliced and cut to increase air flow or to accommodate long fingernails.[20]

Round rubber grippers used to open stuck jar lids will help free needles from fabric.[21] A small surgical needle holder is also a helpful tool. Snap it right on the needle and pull.[22]

An old pair of rubber gloves will give plenty of traction. Cut the tip off the "pinky" finger and wear it on the index finger of the needle-holding hand. It will help pull out overloaded needles, without missing a beat. Unlike other needle grabbers, you don't have to stop and put your needle down to pick up this tool. Plus, it will cushion the index finger.

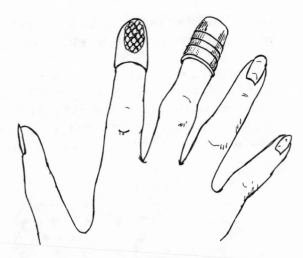

Finger tips from rubber gloves give extra traction.

A thimble with a rubber band wrapped around it is also very handy,[23] just get used to pulling needles out with the "thimbled" finger.

For a better grip on the needle, moisten fingers with Tacky-Finger®, a substance used by bank tellers and other paper shufflers that does just what the name implies.[24]

Beginning

Whenever possible, try to anchor knots in seam allowances. They will be much less likely to pop out.

Getting a healthy-sized knot to pass through a quilt top by just tugging at it is risky business. Instead, pop it through by stroking the knot with your thumbnail in one direction as you pull the thread in the other. If, after two or three tries, the knot doesn't pop right in, it's probably a little too big. Cut it off and make a smaller one.

After the knot goes through, there may be a small "hole" where the threads of the fabric have moved apart. To return the fabric to its original state, gently scratch the "hole" in several directions with your fingernail.

To begin without a knot, insert the needle one needle's length away from the point where the first stitch will be taken on the proposed line of stitching. Bring the point up to begin the first stitch, and pull all of the thread through, save for a short tail.

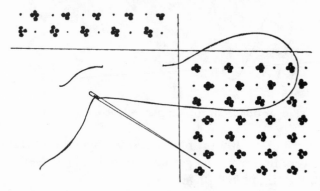

Begin about an inch away, leaving a small tail.

As the first few stitches are taken, they will catch the thread placed in their path earlier, either by actually piercing it, or by passing very close to either side.

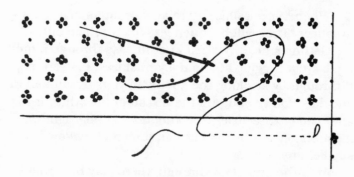

Quilt towards the tail, over the thread.

As the quilting stitches approach the tail, give the tail a little tug. If it feels loose, pull the thread out and begin again. If not, consider it secure and clip the tail.[25]

To cut down on starting and stopping, cut off twice the length of thread normally used. Don't knot it, just pull half of it through the quilt on the first stitch, leaving a long tail. Quilt as usual, end, and then re-thread with the tail and continue quilting.[26] This is especially effective when working on a frame and the quilt can't be turned to accommodate a favorite quilting position. By leaving tails and coming back to finish them, even the most complicated quilting strategies can be sewn with the fewest threads.

If long tails get in the way, stick a long pin in the quilt, and wrap the thread around from point to head, securing the last little bit around the head. Remove the pin and the thread will be crimped, but ready to go, and without tangles. Pins should be placed parallel to the long side of the quilt if it is to be rolled before the pin is released.

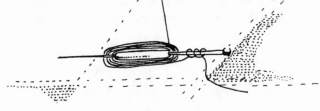

Pin long tails out of the way.

Ending

Not particularly adept at making a knot at the surface of the quilt? Try knotting around a corsage pin. Stick the pin very near the last stitch and tie a knot around it. Do it again, this time lifting the first knot up and out of the way before pulling the second one taught. Remove the pin and pop the knot.

After ending a line of stitching with a knot, leave a long tail. Take a corsage pin, and swish it around under the top, pulling in the tail. In case the knot ever pops out, there will be something to thread to sneak it back in.

The slickest trick for ending a line of stitching without a knot is to weave the thread between the last few stitches, under the top. Begin by sliding the point of the needle into the quilt through the hole from which the thread is exiting. Have the point exit the quilt above the line of stitching. Grab the point and pull the eye and thread into the quilt but not out again. While the eye is under the top, slide it between the last two stitches showing on the top, aiming for an area below the line of stitching. Pop the eye out by rubbing the fabric over the eye with the inside of the thumbnail. (This will ease it through without making a hole.) Grab the eye and pull the point into the quilt but not out again. Guide the point between the next two stitches. Continue weaving the thread between the stitches until enough resistance is felt to reassure you that it won't come out. The smaller the stitches, the less weaving is required.[27]

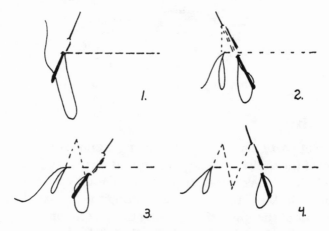

Weaving the thread to end a line of stitching.

You can also begin a line of stitching with this technique. To avoid skipped stitches on continuous lines of quilting, such as feather veins, cables, etc., modify the technique just slightly. Begin the new thread by leaving a small space before taking the first stitch, and leave a tail. After the line of quilting has been sewn, come back and re-thread the beginning. This time, however, instead of entering in the hole from which the thread is exiting, take a "fake stitch" through the top and batting but not through the lining, over the space left earlier. Bring the point up, but not the eye, and continue weaving as described above. If this technique is used to begin and end lines of stitching, there will be no "skipped" stitches visible on either the top or the back.[28]

Traveling

The best way to get from one part of a quilting motif to the next is to use both the eye and the point of the needle to travel under the quilt top. It's the ideal solution when the distance to travel is greater than the length of the needle. Enter the hole from which the thread is exiting with the point of the needle. Slide the point under the top with the thimble and bring out the point. (It will look like one long stitch.) Pull the point as far as possible *without pulling the eye of the needle out of the quilt.* Now turn the needle 180°, still keeping the eye under the quilt top. Now lead with the eye. Push the eye under the top and out of the quilt, while leaving the point in, turn it and lead with the point. You can travel indefinitely under the top without ever pulling the needle all the way out of the quilt![29]

Ripping

If stitches need to come out, slide the needle off the thread and loosen each stitch with the eye of the needle, one stitch at a time. Don't loosen stitches with the point of the needle as it might inadvertently split the thread or, worse yet, catch part of the fabric.

Disposable stitch removers (make friends with a nurse) are good for catching the thread and then cutting it.[30]

Before stitching through the same place again, scratch the place on the quilt where the stitches came out with a fingernail to return the weave of the cloth and batting fibers to as near their original position as possible. This will keep the needle from accidently falling into one of the previous holes, and make it less likely to run into a waiting finger down below. By closing holes, the needle will act more predictably and can be guided with equal force through all stitches.

Tidying Up

Keep a damp washrag on a plate near your chair, and deposit loose threads on it as they are cut from the quilt. The threads will stick to the cloth for easy disposal later, rather than attaching to you, the carpeting, or your cat.[31]

A small piece of batting laid on the quilt is also a good place to put thread ends. (Of course there's always the floor!)[32]

Wiping the quilt top with a chunk of batting will pick up any forgotten threads.[33] Masking tape rolled sticky side out on the edge of your chair or table will hold on to those loose threads, too.[34] Want something a little more high-tech? Keep a rechargeable Dustbuster® handy to suck up stray threads.[35]

Clip loose threads with a pair of scissors that have rounded tips, especially if the scissors lay directly on the quilt between snips.[36]

Stray threads between top and batting can be removed with a corsage pin. Slide the corsage pin

between the top and batting, and position it under the
stray thread. With a steady hand and a light touch,
scrape the point of the pin against the top of the quilt.
When the point comes to the thread, change the angle
of the pin slightly to push the thread out between the
weave of the cloth. When the tip of the pin and the
thread are visible, take the point of a quilting needle
and pick at the thread until it comes away from the
pin. When a tiny loop of thread appears, remove the corsage pin, and pull the stray thread out.

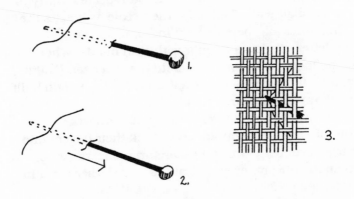

Remove stray threads with a corsage pin.

Hand pieced seam allowances can be maneuvered
to make quilting easier even after the quilt has been
basted. Shine a flashlight up through the quilt to locate
the seam allowance first, then use a corsage pin to wig-
gle it into place.

Finding Lost Needles

Finding stray needles lodged in high pile carpeting
is best achieved by getting your face down on the floor
and shining a flashlight over the area. Look for the
reflection, and try not to stick your face.[37]

You can troll for stray pins and needles by slowly moving a magnetic pin catcher over the floor. A clicking sound indicates you've found one.

Large veterinary magnets, the kind cows swallow, can be rolled across an area suspected of harboring sharp metal objects.[38]

When all else fails, invite your spouse to walk across the floor barefoot.

Sore Fingers

Alternate bottom fingers to avoid repeated injury to a single digit while feeling for the needle as it exits the lining. After all, there's safety in numbers.

Better yet, learn to quilt with *both* hands. When one set of fingers gets sore, switch to the other set. Quilting with both hands also makes it much easier to stitch difficult angles on a large frame.[39]

To avoid painful pricks, many quilters wear thimbles on their bottom hand, tuck their fingers into parts of rubber gloves and secretarial fingers, wrap them in adhesive or electrical tape, or slather them in clear nail polish![40]

Protect the finger that works under the quilt with NewSkin® before quilting. It gives protection without loss of touch, and if it gets into an open wound, it's much safer than nail polish.[41]

Bag Balm antiseptic, the smelly, gooey stuff intended for cow's udders, relieves sore fingers, too. It can be purchased in the large economy size for cows, or the small personal one ounce tin for quilters.

Chap Stick® lip balm is also soothing on pricked fingers.[42]

Styptic pencil will keep bleeding to a minimum and will relieve soreness, too.[43]

Dampen sore fingers and rub them over a bar of soap before bed. Just don't suck your fingers![44]

Toughen sore fingers in alum or men's after shave lotion.[45]

Soak sore fingers in warm water with Johnson's™ foot soap. After soaking, smooth callouses with a pumice stone.[46]

Soothe rough fingers with a homemade hand lotion consisting of one pound Unibase Ointment™, 16 ounces glycerin, and five cups distilled water. Mix *slowly*, in a *large* bowl, as this stuff expands and tends to foam if mixing is too enthusiastic. Yields three quarts.[47]

Smooth rough skin, relieve sore fingers, and help stimulate callous growth with equal parts of Bacitracin Ointment, Vitamin A and D Ointment, and any cuticle cream. Rub this mixture into fingers every time they get wet, and after each sewing session. It is recommended that you make a "patch test" with each of the ingredients to make sure that you are not allergic to them. Place a small dollop on an adhesive bandage and wear it on the crook of your arm overnight. If the area is red or sore, don't use it in your mixture.[48]

Soreness in the finger tips can be reduced with a massage regimen beginning three days before stitching. Massage for two minutes every two hours.[49]

Machine Quilting

Baste quilts thoroughly, and use a "walking" or "even feed" foot. It will keep all three layers of the quilt moving together at the same rate of speed.

Machine quilting, like hand quilting, requires some forethought. It is helpful to locate the best places to start and stop each line of stitching BEFORE sewing. This is especially true of machine quilting when a continuous line design is desirable. To rehearse, transfer the quilting motif to a piece of paper and trace the quilting strategy with a pencil, then stitch.[50]

Bicycle clips, usually worn to keep pant legs from getting tangled in spokes and gears, can keep quilts from unrolling as they are maneuvered in and out of the sewing machine.[51]

No need to backstitch to begin a line of stitching on the machine. Instead, start sewing with the stitch length set at zero. As the first 1/2" is sewn, slowly dial the stitch length to a normal-sized stitch. To end, dial back down to zero. Clip top and bottom threads at the fabric, and don't worry. It won't come out![52]

Some very fine threads, like nylon machine quilting thread and some silk threads, need to be "lifted" off the spool rather than pulled. To make a "thread lifter," put a flexible plastic drinking straw on the spare spool spindle, providing your machine has one, and bend the straw. Punch a hole with a paper punch near the end of the straw and pass the thread through the hole as the machine is threaded.[53]

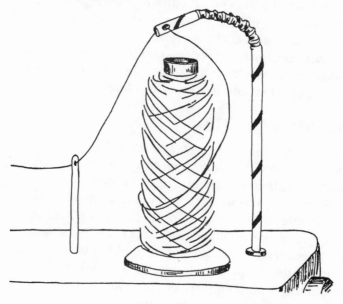

A "thread lifter."

Chapter Notes

[1]Marjorie Kerr, in "Top Tips," *Quilter's Newsletter Magazine*, #25 (November 1971) p. 15.

[2]Aloyse Yorko: Bokeelia, FL.

[3]Betty Salazar: Ft. Worth, TX.

[4]Emma Grandmaison, in "Dear Denise...Your Quilting Tips Column," *Quilt World Omnibook*, Winter 1985, p. 4.

[5]Ibid.

[6]Lavan Lofgren, in "Dear Denise...Your Quilting Tips Column," *Quilt World Omnibook*, Winter 1985, p. 4.

[7]Kathi Buckner: Center Line, MI.

[8]"200 Top Tips," *Quilter's Newsletter Magazine*, #200 (March 1988) p. 67.

[9]Judy Tescher, in "Top Tips," *Quilter's Newsletter Magazine*, #199 (February 1988) p. 46.

[10]"200 Top Tips," *Quilter's Newsletter Magazine*, #200 (March 1988) p. 66.

[11]Barbara Bannister, in "Questions & Answers," *Quilt World*, November/December 1981, p. 7.

[12]Phyllis Klein: Warwick, NY.

[13]Berthe Given, in "Top Tips," *Quilter's Newsletter Magazine*, #171 (April 1985) p. 51.

[14]Gail Chatterson: Howell, MI.

[15]Helen W. Rose, "Pins, Needles, Thread And Knots For Patchwork," *Quilt World*, November/December 1981, p. 7.

[16]Phyllis Klein: Warwick, NY. From an anonymous quilter.

[17]Mrs. Forest Lemaster, in "Letters To The Editor," *Quilt World*, March/April 1982, p. 5.

[18]Kay Weygandt: Akron, OH. Shared by Fran Drosenos: Cuyahoga Falls, OH.

[19]Bonnie Ellis: Minneapolis, MN.

[20]Glynda J. Malleske: Austin, TX.

[21]Muriel Hornig, in "Notes & Quotes," *Quilt World*, July/August 1982, p. 42.

[22]Mabel J. Hartley: Menasha, WI.

[23]Mrs. David C. Trigg, in "Top Tips," *Quilter's Newsletter Magazine*, #98 (January 1978) p. 29.

[24]Holice Turnbow: Sheperdstown, WV.

[25] Cathy Grafton: Pontiac, IL.

[26] Peggy Greene: Indianapolis, IN.

[27] Phyllis Klein: Warwick, NY.

[28] Adapted from a technique shown to me by Amy Bunce: Wauconda, IL.

[29] Eileen Cameron: NJ. Shared by Phyllis Klein: Warwick, NY.

[30] Mabel J. Hartley: Menasha, WI.

[31] Margot Strand Jensen: Denver, CO.

[32] Odette Teel: Long Beach, CA.

[33] Helen Kelley: Minneapolis, MN.

[34] "200 Top Tips," *Quilter's Newsletter Magazine*, #200 (March 1988) p. 67.

[35] Caron Mosey: Flushing, MI.

[36] "100 Top Tips," *Quilter's Newsletter Magazine*, #100 (March 1978) p. 14.

[37] Odette Teel: Long Beach, CA.

[38] From a former student.

[39] Jinny Beyer: Great Falls, VA.

[40] Pat Morris, "Quilter's Queries & Quotes," *Quilt World*, January 1989, p. 22-23.

[41] Barbara Bannister, in "Questions & Answers," *Quilt World*, November/December 1982, p. 18.

[42] Sharyn Craig: San Diego, CA.

[43] "200 Top Tips," *Quilter's Newsletter Magazine*, #200 (March 1988) p. 10.

[44] Arlone Ritter: Blue Mound, IL.

[45] Pat Morris, "Questions & Answers," *Quilt World*, July/August 1981, p. 23.

[46] Diana Boufford: Windsor, Ontario.

[47] Betty Salazar: Ft. Worth, TX.

[48] Dr. Susan Delaney-Mech, "Prescription For Quilters," *Quilt World*, November/December 1987, p. 6.

[49] Ibid.

[50] Anita Murphy: Kountze, TX.

[51] Harriet Hargrave, *Heirloom Machine Quilting* (Westminster, CA: Burdett Design Studios, 1987) p. 21.

[52] Ibid., p. 10. Shared by Caryl Bryer Fallert: Oswego, IL.

[53] Sharyn Craig: San Diego, CA.

CHAPTER THIRTEEN
BINDING AND FINISHING

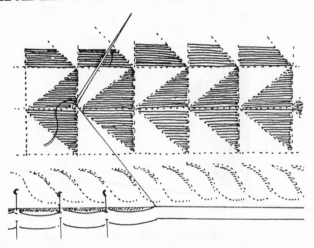

Continuous Bias Binding

Begin with a square of fabric. Put identifying marks on the top and bottom sides, and cut the square diagonally, forming two triangles.

Identify top and bottom; cut diagonally.

With right sides together, join the triangles along the marked sides with a 1/4" seam. Press.

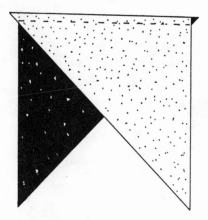

Join with a 1/4" seam.

On the wrong side, mark parallel lines along the longest side. These lines should be the same distance apart as the width of the binding. (Try 2 1/2" for folded binding.) If the distance between the last line and the bottom edge does not equal the width of the binding, trim it to the line above.

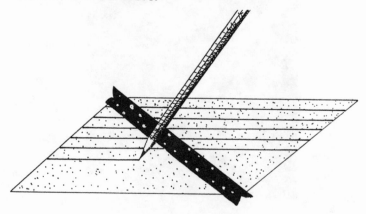

Mark lines on long side.

With right sides together, bring the two short sides together and pin so that the first marked line is even with the raw edge. All other lines should match, save for the last, which is again even with a raw edge. It will look like a tube that is "off" by one width. Join with a 1/4" seam, press, and cut along the marked lines.[1]

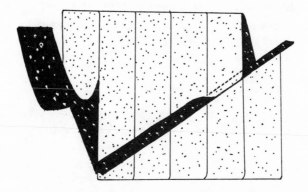

Bring short sides together, matching first line
with raw edge. Stitch, press, cut.

When making narrow strips of bias binding use a short, tight stitch. This will keep them from coming apart once they are cut.[2]

To calculate the bias yield (in inches) of any square, divide the length of one side by the width of the bias strip. Then multiply that number by the side of the square.[3]

Keeping Things Organized

To keep bias strips from tangling, lay them out on the ironing board and roll them around a cardboard tube from a roll of paper towels. Hang the tube on a coat hanger and unroll as needed.[4]

Support a large quilt during machine stitching on either a large table or in the arms of a friend.[5]

Corners And Joins

To sew binding with mitered corners that are folded
instead of sewn, pin binding to the quilt, matching raw
edges, and stitch 1/4" from the edge as usual. Stop
stitching 1/4" from the bottom edge, backstitch to secure stitching, and remove the quilt from the machine.
Bring binding to the next side, folding the binding at
the corner and matching raw edges along the side. The
fold should meet the raw edge of the last side sewn.
Pin. Insert the needle 1/4" from the top of the quilt and
resume sewing.[6]

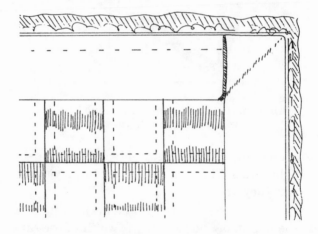

Bring binding to the next side and
fold at right angle.

There are actually two folds made by the binding at
the corner. One is visible, lines up with the raw edge,
and forms a right angle at the top of the quilt. The
other is hidden under the fold of the first and runs diagonally. Feel for it and push your fingernail alongside it
to make an indentation in the fabric. Place the sewing
machine needle on the indentation exactly 1/4" from
the edge of the quilt for perfect corners.

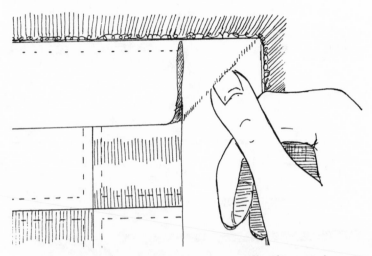

Mark the unseen fold for correct needle placement.

To complete the binding with a mitered seam, leave a 6" tail of binding and begin sewing about 4" from the middle of one side. After the fourth corner is sewn, plan to stop sewing about 4" from the middle of this last side, leaving another 6" tail and about 8" of quilt with no binding attached. Take the quilt out of the machine, lay it on a flat surface, and smooth the tails in place even with the edge of the quilt. Cut the tail on the right diagonally now, if this has not been done previously. Lay the cut right tail over the left one, and, using the cut edge of the right tail as a guide, mark a diagonal line on the left tail. Move the two tails apart. On the right tail, mark a line 1/4" to the right of the raw edge. This will be the sewing line. On the left tail, mark a line 1/2" to the right of the line made earlier. This will be the cutting line. Cut on the cutting line, bring right sides together with raw edges even, and sew on the sewing line. Pin binding to quilt to make sure all this has been done correctly before sewing this last part of the binding to the quilt.

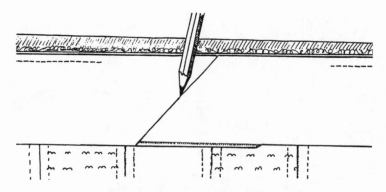

Mark a diagonal line on the left tail.

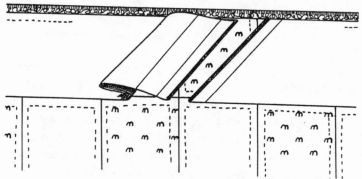

Mark a sewing line on the right tail.

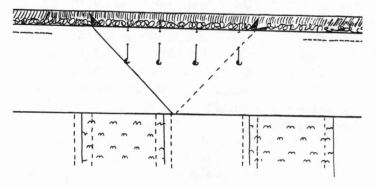

Pin in place to assure proper fit.

Stitching And Signing

To machine stitch a binding "in the ditch" from the right side, roll the binding to the back, and place pins on top *parallel* to the edge. By pinning parallel, not perpendicular, the binding won't shift out of place. Remove pins just before the presser foot hits them.[7]

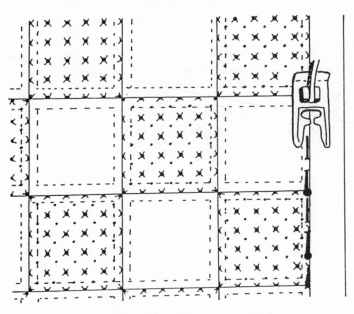

Pin parallel, and stitch in the ditch.

Use waste canvas to make perfect cross stitch signatures. Dampen and remove after stitching.[8]

Historical information, pertinent facts about the quilt, even laundering instructions can be typed onto a piece of starched muslin and stitched to the lining of the quilt.[9] It can also be attached with snaps for easier removal when the quilt is washed.

Chapter Notes

[1]Jo Carpenter, "Quilter's Notebook: Continuous Bias," *Quilt World*, December 1978, p. 34.

[2]Julie Hussar: Linden, MI.

[3]Jo Carpenter, "Quilter's Notebook: Continuous Bias," *Quilt World*, December 1978, p. 34.

[4]Wanda Redding, in "Top Tips," *Quilter's Newsletter Magazine*, #197 (November/December 1987) p. 70.

[5]"200 Top Tips," *Quilter's Newsletter Magazine*, #200 (March 1988) p. 11.

[6]Judy Anne Walter: Evanston, IL.

[7]Suggested by Nancy Jacoby: Wabash, IN. Featured in Harriet Hargrave, *Heirloom Machine Quilting* (Westminster, CA: Burdett Design Studios, 1987) p. 39.

[8]Elly Sienkiewicz: Washington, D.C.

[9]"200 Top Tips," *Quilter's Newsletter Magazine*, #200 (March 1988) p. 11.

CHAPTER FOURTEEN
QUILT CARE

Washing Quilts

Quilts are best laundered in cold water, with a mild soap and very little agitation. A bathtub, scrubbed clean, is an ideal place to gently wash even the largest quilt. Make sure the soap is completely dissolved before the quilt is placed in the water, and rinse the quilt at least twice. After the final rinse, gently push the quilt against the side of the tub to let more water out, then carefully scoop it into a plastic laundry basket for the trip to the washing machine. A short spin will remove most of the water without stressing the stitches.

Wet quilts can be lifted out of the tub more easily by placing several rolled bath towels under the quilt. Lift the towels and the quilt will follow.[1]

A child's wading pool is a good place to wash quilts, especially if they will be dried outside.[2]

Dry freshly laundered quilts outside on an old sheet, bright side down. Cover the back with a thin sheet to protect it from sunlight and passing birds.

During inclement weather, quilts can also be dried indoors on a layer of towels, either on the bed or floor. Fold the quilt one or two times to save space. About every hour, re-fold the quilt in a different direction, changing the towels if necessary. This will speed up the drying process and will keep the quilt from drying with hard crease marks.

Wall quilts can be hung when still damp. In fact, they will hang flatter if allowed to dry on the wall. If there is a rod pocket at the bottom they can also be weighted with a thin, lightweight dowel.

After laundering, most quilts will look a little wrinkled. To smooth these small wrinkles, just sleep under the quilt for a few nights!

Vacuum quilts too fragile to wash through a piece of nylon net with one of the hand-held attachments. If the vacuum has a low speed, use it.

To remove pet hair or clinging threads, take a few swipes with a lint roller. The masking tape won't damage the quilt, and it will pick up a surprising amount. Quilts should be "taped" before they are sent off to competition, too.

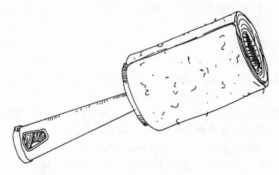

A lint roller removes stray threads and pet hair.

Wiping the quilt while wearing rubber gloves is effective, too.[3]

Removing Stains

Blood stains can be removed by sponging with an ice cube. Mop and sponge until the stain is gone.[4]

Saliva will also remove blood stains. As with any remedy it is best to get at the stain before it sets. Saliva contains various enzymes which break down foodstuffs when we eat. These enzymes are relatively broad-based and act on a variety of different things, including proteins. Because blood contains a sizeable amount of protein, it, too, can be broken down or dissolved by the enzymes found in saliva. By the way, the saliva need not come from the same person as the blood.[5]

Meat tenderizer containing *papain* (from papaya) mixed with water to form a paste will also remove blood stains.[6] Peroxide will work, too.[7] It should be rinsed out immediately, however, as it may bleach the fabric.

Ink from ball point pens is best removed with cheap hair spray. Saturate the area and blot. Repeat as many times as necessary, then wash out the hair spray.[8]

Brown age spots can be removed with little damage to the quilt by soaking the affected areas in a mixture of one quart buttermilk, one tablespoon vinegar, and one gallon water. Repeat as necessary.[9] Rinse treated areas afterwards.

Rust spots can be removed by sponging lemon juice on the spot and holding it over a steaming kettle.[10] Keep your fingers and your quilt well away from the hot kettle (and from the burner) to avoid injury to you or the quilt. Rinse the quilt thoroughly after treatment and be advised that this procedure may weaken the fabric of old or well-worn quilts.

Removing Leftover Markings

Cheap hair spray will also remove pencil marks. Lightly spray the area, allow to dry, and rub with a clean gum eraser.[11]

A Pentel Click Eraser (ZE-21) is easy to hold on to and removes pencil marks. Replacement eraser sticks to fit the plastic holder are also available.[12]

To get at offending pencil marks, slip a pin under the line to lift it up from the batting. This will keep the eraser from needlessly rubbing on the rest of the quilt.[13]

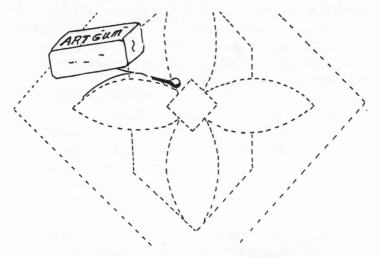

Slip a pin under the pencil line, then erase.

A solution of three tablespoons alcohol, one tablespoon water, two drops of liquid dishwashing detergent (yellow, not green) will also remove pencil marks. Rinse thoroughly.[14]

Rub white and silver pencil lines off without damaging the quilt with a wad of quilt batting.[15]

The best way to remove the blue markings left by water soluble pens is to submerge the entire quilt in a very clean bathtub filled with cold water. Leave it there for several hours. Spraying the marks "away" with a plant mister only wicks them into the batting to reappear later. Never wash these markings out with laundry detergent as some kinds of detergent will set the marks brown, permanently.

Always read the instructions on the package, and test each fabric to be used BEFORE marking.

As an extra safeguard when using water soluble pens, give all quilting fabric a double rinse. Since chemicals in these markers react with chemicals in some laundry detergents, make sure there are no detergent residues left on the fabric after pre-washing.

The blue marks from commercially stamped kits can be removed at the dry cleaners with Streetex and Picrin.[16] In the trade it's called a "two-one" treatment, which refers to the ratio of Streetex to Picrin.[17]

Some marked lines, especially those from wax-based chalk pencils, need to be coaxed off the fabric with gentle rubbing. Always rub with a piece of cloth of the same color, in case the rubbing accidently becomes too strenuous. Colors from one piece of fabric can be rubbed onto the other.

Chapter Notes

[1]Annie Putnam, "Tips And Brilliant Ideas," *Canada Quilts*, Vol. XVII, No. 5 (November 1988) p. 28.

[2]Alice Freeman, in "Top Tip," *Quilter's Newsletter Magazine*, #204 (July/August 1988) p. 37.

[3]Beebe Moss: Southfield, MI.

[4]Helen Kelley: Minneapolis, MN. Recommended by The British Quilter's Guild.

[5]Dr. David O'Keeffe, Department of Chemistry, University of Michigan-Flint.

[6]*Eastern Long Island Quilters' Guild Newsletter*, Southampton, NY.

[7]Betty Jo Shiell: Tallahassee, FL.

[8]Ginny Bennetter: Garden City, NY.

[9]*The Ohio Valley Star*, as cited in "Some Nifty Ideas From Quilters," *Patchwork Patter*, #55 (August 1986) p. 13.

[10]"Some Nifty Ideas From Quilters," *Patchwork Patter*, #55 (August 1986) p. 13.

[11]Marie Spriggs: Dallas, TX.

[12]Anita Murphy: Kountze, TX.

[13]Bea Walwroth, in "Tips And Brilliant Ideas," *Canada Quilts*, Vol. XVII, No. 5 (November 1988) p. 28.

[14]Helen Kelley: Minneapolis, MN.

[15]Anita Murphy: Kountze, TX.

[16]Mary Conroy: Sudbury, Ontario.

[17]Christine Tithof, Pro-Clean Professional Dry Cleaners, Grand Blanc, MI.

CHAPTER FIFTEEN
DISPLAY AND STORAGE

Hanging Methods

When making rod pockets, fold the raw edges of the pocket together and baste it to the top of the quilt before sewing on the binding. In this way, only one length of the pocket needs to be hand sewn.[1]

To make a rod pocket that will not distort the quilt once the rod is in place, cut a strip of fabric double the finished width of the pocket plus 1/2", and as long as the quilt is wide. Hem both short sides. Fold widthwise so that the raw edges meet in the middle, wrong side in. Press to make a sharp crease along each edge. With wrong sides together, join raw edges with a 1/4" seam. Sew the seamed side against the quilt, along the pressed creases. Because of the fabric taken up in the seam, the pocket will bulge slightly on the back, but the rod will not show from the front of the quilt.[2]

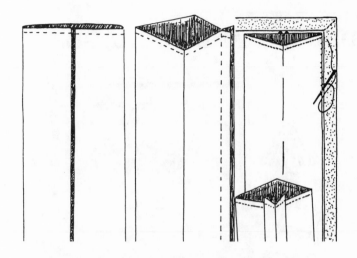

A non-distorting rod pocket.

A rod pocket can be placed on the bottom of a quilt, too. A second pocket with a lightweight rod will help the quilt hang straight without curling.

Large quilts can be hung using a length of electrical conduit and two or three eye screws. It is much stronger than a wood dowel of the same diameter and will not sag as much.

One-and-three-quarter inch wide flat galvanized steel strips may bow slightly under the weight of large heavy quilts, but otherwise they are virtually indiscernible, as quilts appear to be flush against the wall. They come with 3/8" diameter holes spaced 3/4" apart, and can be found in the "do-it-yourself" section of most hardware stores. Cut longer than the rod pocket, but shorter than the width of the quilt.

Inch wide wooden lattice stripping can be used to hang quilts, and does not show when the quilt is hung. Cut the lattice strips slightly shorter than the width of the quilt, but just a little longer than the rod pocket. Bore little holes at each end. Slip the rod into the rod

pocket and hang with thin nails. If the quilt is large and
the lattice stripping needs support in the middle, sew
the rod pocket in two parts, separated by about 1/2".
Bore one hole in each end and one in the middle. To
balance the quilt, suspend it from the middle first, then
balance the two sides.[3]

To keep the lattice stripping from rolling, bore the
holes near the upper edge instead of in the middle.[4]

Miniature quilts can be hung with safety pins if a
rod and rod pocket add noticeable bulk. Insert two
safety pins vertically into the backing of the quilt at the
upper corners, placing the circle sides towards the top.
Tap two nails into the wall and loop the safety pins over
the nail heads.[5]

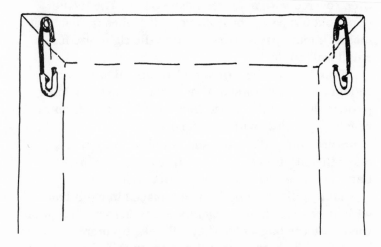

Hang miniature quilts with safety pins.

Rods and rod pockets can be eliminated altogether
by hanging quilts with Velcro®. Sew a long strip of the
fuzzy part (loop side) to the back of the quilt along the
top edge. Staple, glue, or nail its mate (hook side) to a
piece of wood. Hang the wood, then press the two
halves of the Velcro® together. [6]

Display Strategies

To see if an area is suitable for displaying a quilt, take a few pieces of the fabric used in the quilt and put them where the quilt might be displayed. After a few weeks, compare them to the quilt to see what damage, if any, has been wrought by the sun.[7]

Old or valuable quilts should not be displayed continuously. They need time to rest. A good policy is to rotate them every six months: Six months on display, six months in storage.[8]

Storage

The best way to store quilts is rolled on a cardboard tube covered with acid free tissue paper. The tissue paper should cover the quilt as well. Tubes from Christmas wrapping paper are often just the right size for small wall quilts.[9]

If quilts must be stored folded, take them out and re-fold them from time to time, alternating the folding pattern. If originally folded in quarters with the top in, re-fold it in thirds with the top out.

Store quilts in fabric bags or pillow cases which allow them to breathe. Never store quilts in plastic bags, and *never ever* in plastic trash bags.

Some quilts fare better when placed in cloth bags without folding. Instead, gently crumple them and push them into the bag as is. They will take up more room, but will never have deep or permanent folds because of going into the bag the same way each time.

Use the old "nurse trick" for bagging quilts. Turn the bag inside out. With a hand inside the bag, grab the quilt and pull the bag right-side out and over the quilt.[10]

Keep quilts from direct contact with wood. The oils will stain the fabric, and the acids may damage fibers over time.[11]

Chapter Notes

[1] Nancy Halpern: Natick, MA.

[2] Catherine Anthony: Houston, TX. Shared by Marion Vernon: Prospect Heights, IL.

[3] Nancy Halpern: Natick, MA.

[4] Ruth McDowell: Winchester, MA. Shared by Nancy Halpern: Natick, MA.

[5] Debra Radecky: Stow, OH.

[6] "100 Top Tips," *Quilter's Newsletter Magazine,* #100 (March 1978) p. 12.

[7] Jeffrey Gutcheon, "Not For Shop Keepers Only," *Quilter's Newsletter Magazine*, #185 (September 1986) p. 42.

[8] Diane Marvin, "Collecting And Caring For Old Quilts," *Quilt*, Spring 1986, p. 42-43.

[9] Phyllis Klein, "The Great Holiday Cover Up," *Quilt*, Winter 1984, p. 18-19.

[10] Betty Afaganis: Lethbridge, Alberta.

[11] Diane Marvin, "Collecting And Caring For Old Quilts," *Quilt*, Spring 1986, p. 42-43.

CHAPTER SIXTEEN

ORGANIZATION

Notions

To keep plastic tape measures under control, put a gripper snap on the end.

Discarded plastic cannisters from 35mm film make excellent containers in which to store t-pins, paper clips, leftover gripper snaps, grommets, and other small items.[1] Cannisters from Fuji film are clear. Local camera shops will be only too happy to save them for you.

Store small sewing supplies in the plastic drawers intended to organize nuts and bolts.[2]

Fishing tackle boxes make the nicest sewing baskets.[3] But don't stop at quilting supplies. One of the nicest organizers of embroidery floss is a Fenwick™ tackle box. Wrap floss around pieces of cardboard or plastic, and pop them into the little adjustable compartments. The lid is semi-transparent, and the deluxe model is even two-sided![4]

Floss can also be stored quite nicely in plastic pages made to hold 35mm slides. Each page has twenty pockets opening at the top, and three holes along the side so they can be kept in three-ring binders. Wrap floss around pieces of cardboard or plastic the size of the slide pocket, and arrange by color or number.[5]

Plastic three-drawer paper caddies are great for storing thread. Dump out the typing paper and sort spools by color.

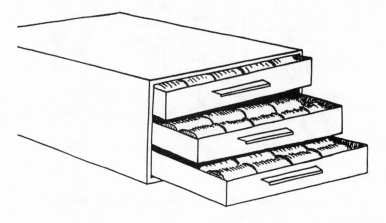

Store thread in paper caddies.

Clear plastic shoe boxes are just the right size for storing ric-rac, commercially made bias tape, and other sewing notions that come wrapped around cardboard cards.[6]

File patterns away in the filing boxes used for home records. The paper accordion style have built in alphabetical dividers and pockets. The plastic ones can be easily outfitted with dividers and file folders.[7]

Go big time and invest in a two-drawer filing cabinet. There will be room enough for patterns, some quilting stencils, class notes, templates, magazine articles, and photographs.[8]

Empty laundry detergent boxes with the lids and part of one side cut off can be covered with pretty paper and used to store quilting magazines.[9]

Wooden yardsticks come in 48" lengths, too. Doesn't just knowing that make your heart beat a little faster?

Fabric

Make it a habit to pre-wash and press all fabric as soon as it comes home from the quilt shop. It's much more efficient than stopping in the middle of something to do it, especially once the creative juices have started to flow.[10]

Measure then fold fabric after pre-washing, and stick a piece of masking tape on the top corner recording the yardage and other important information.[11]

Cut the opening and part of one side off of plastic gallon milk containers, and load them with fat quarters and fabric sticks according to color. Set them on a shelf, handle side out. When needed, carry them to the work table a gallon at a time!

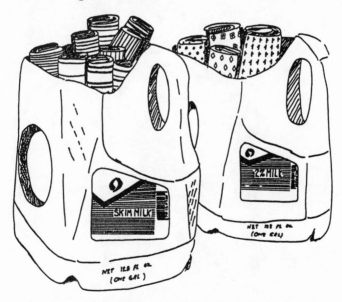

Store fat quarters in gallon milk containers.

Store fabric less than a yard long in wheeled vegetable carts. The models with removable drawers are the most handy. Pull out a drawer at a time, or wheel the whole thing over to the work table.

Smaller scraps can be sorted by color family and kept in plastic storage baskets.[12]

Work In Progress

When starting a quilt project, prepare a box in which to store all the cut pieces, extra fabric, templates, any notes, directions, etc. Label the outside of the box with the name of the project. This way, if the project is ongoing over a long period of time, there is no risk of accidently appropriating needed fabric for another project.[13]

Clip finished blocks to a skirt hanger to keep them wrinkle free and out of the way.[14]

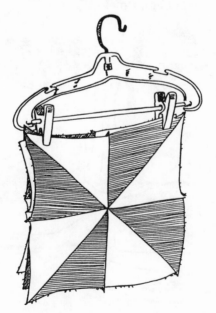

Skirt hangers keep blocks wrinkle free.

Work Areas

Keep a complete set of tools for each work area. If you have your own sewing room, but sometimes stitch in the living room, there should be a second set of supplies there, too.[15]

Rest quilting books in plastic recipe book holders so stitching and reading don't have to be mutually exclusive.[16]

Roll from sewing machine to ironing board to work table on wheels with a steno chair.[17]

Steno chairs get you from here to there.

A 3' x 5' plywood board covered with heavy canvas stretched over a doubled mattress pad makes a wonderful surface for ironing, cutting, and pinning.[18]

A plywood board measuring 40" x 70" can be covered with a folding cardboard cutting mat, giving a 1" gridded work surface, complete with ruler, diagonal lines for cutting on the bias, and scallop guides. Scribble notes on it, stick pins into it, and when it gets ratty looking, replace it with another.

Plywood, without the cardboard cutting mat, is a good working surface on its own.[19]

Thinking big? Ping-Pong tables are great work surfaces, too.[20]

Paperwork

Document and photograph every quilt. Record title, date completed, dimensions, materials, technique, and any other important information. Do this for insurance purposes and for those who come after you.

Keep envelopes handy when reading quilting magazines. If the urge to order strikes, address the envelope on the spot and write the amount due on the inside flap.

Flag interesting magazine articles or often-referenced pages in quilting books with little yellow Post-it™ notes. They are easily removed, won't harm the paper, and will save you from hours of time paging through back issues trying to find something.[21]

Travel

Keep a travel kit filled with essential sewing supplies for on-the-go sewing. When you leave home, pop in a small project and matching thread.[22]

Don't use sewing supplies from the travel kit unless you are away from home, especially if there's a chance something won't get put back. Hunting down tools ahead of time, and keeping track of them is a real time saver.[23]

Workshops

The urge is always to pack everything that's not nailed down, in case you'll need it. Most of the smaller things will fit in a hanging cosmetic case with clear plastic zippered pockets. Take out the hanger to make more room. Look for cosmetic cases in department stores right before Mother's Day and Christmas.

Don't try to go through airport security with 8" sewing shears in your purse. Carry smaller folding scissors instead.

Small scissors that don't fold should be sheathed during transit. Cotton balls or a piece of cork at the points will keep work safe from accidental holes and slashes.[24]

Trim return address labels and glue them to the tops of thread spools for easy identification. Then throw a couple extra in your tote bag. They make exchanging addresses with new friends simpler, and they save time when filling out raffle tickets.

Glue a sheet of sandpaper inside a manila file folder for a portable non-slip work surface. The sandpaper will stay flat in the folder, and when the file folder is closed, the sandpaper won't cling to anything it's not supposed to.[25]

Keep a three-ring binder for notes taken while attending workshops, and bring a hole punch to class. If there are any handouts from the instructor, you can punch holes and organize on the spot.[26]

Bring along an extra handful of fat quarters to trade with other quilters.[27]

Few hotels, and hardly any dorm rooms, have light bright enough to sew by. Bring your own 150 watt light bulb.[28]

Pass out "freebies" to conference participants with a pre-addressed envelope bearing the name of the donor. That way recipients can dash off thank you notes quickly and painlessly.[29]

Miscellaneous Tip

So as not to stop quilting, appliqueing, or piecing in order to eat, keep a bag of M&M's® (either plain or peanut) by your side as you stitch.[30]

Chapter Notes

[1] Judy Florence: Eau Claire, WI.

[2] Donna Maki: Holt, MI.

[3] Pat Morris, "The Mavericks In My Quilting Basket," *Quilt World*, May/June 1980, p. 8.

[4] Deb Nicholson: Ortonville, MI.

[5] Mary Loesch, in "Helps & Hints," *Craft Art Needlework Digest*, April 1988, p. 61.

[6] Odette Teel: Long Beach, CA.

[7] Anita Murphy, "O Is For Organization," *Quilt Almanac*, 1984, p. 44.

[8] Betsy Hatch: Arcadia, CA.

[9] Beebe Moss: Southfield, MI.

[10] "Quick Quilting Tips," *Quilt*, Winter 1988, p. 21.

[11] "Helpful Hints," *Creative Quilting*, May/June 1987, p. 82.

[12] "Quick Quilting Tips," *Quilt*, Winter 1988, p. 21.

[13] Sharyn Craig: San Diego, CA.

[14] Pat Morris, "The Mavericks In My Quilting Basket," *Quilt World*, May/June 1980, p. 8.

[15] Betsy Hatch, "There's Never Enough Time," *Quilt*, Spring 1986, p. 28.

[16] Lois Smith: Rockville, MD.

[17] Mabel J. Hartley: Menasha, WI.

[18] Imogene Gooch, in "Helpful Hints From Indiana Quilters," *Lady's Circle Patchwork Quilts*, February/March 1987, p. 62.

[19] Louise Regan: Ann Arbor, MI.

[20] Donna Maki: Holt, MI.

[21] Jean Ray Laury: Clovis, CA.

[22] Nancy Halpern: Natick, MA.

[23] Sharyn Craig: San Diego, CA.

[24] Pat Morris, "The Mavericks In My Quilting Basket," *Quilt World*, May/June 1980, p. 8.

[25] Eunice Risberg, as cited by Jean Pell, "Tools Of The Trade," *Quilt World*, January/February 1984, p. 28.

[26] Sharyn Craig: San Diego, CA.

[27] "Quick Quilting Tips," *Quilt*, Winter 1988, p. 21.

[28] Kay Lukasko: Cinnaminson, NJ.

[29] Donna Gollehon: Bozeman, MT.

[30] Margot Strand Jensen: Denver, CO.

CHAPTER SEVENTEEN
TIPS TOO GOOD TO PASS UP

Sewing-Related Tips

When sewing buttons on by machine, it's often difficult to position them under the presser foot. To keep
them from sliding around, *tape* them in place with
transparent tape which can be removed when the job is
done.[1]

To make gathers on the machine, pull a length of
thread from the needle towards you, just slightly longer
than the fabric to be gathered. Lay the thread on top of
the fabric and zigzag over it. Take the fabric out of the
machine, and pull the thread.[2] For longer pieces of fabric, zigzag over kite string or button hole twist.[3]

To coax the presser foot over a thick seam, place a
piece of folded fabric under the back of the foot to keep
it level and feeding normally.[4]

Use a wet toothbrush to hold seams down and open
when pressing. Run it just ahead of the iron.[5]

REALLY MISCELLANEOUS TIPS

Thump the hard end of a head of iceberg lettuce against the side of the sink to remove the core.[6]

When static electricity flattens your hair to your head, gently rub your hair back into place with a dryer sheet.[7] Take a sheet with you when you go shopping to restore your coiffure after trying on clothes. You can also rub a dryer sheet up and down your legs to release the hold your pantyhose may have suddenly developed on clingy skirts and dresses.

Use pantyhose to line dry sweaters. Pin the waistband to the line, thread the legs through the neck and out the sleeves, and then pin the feet to the line.[8]

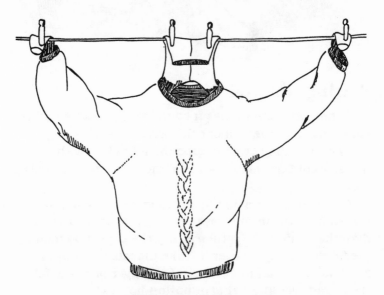

Line dry sweaters a new way.

Drop your Grabbit™ (heavy magnetic pin catcher) down the leg of an old pair of panty hose and dangle it behind the stove or refrigerator to retrieve lost spatulas and other interesting metal objects.

Fishing.

Chapter Notes

[1]Freda Crary: Jordan, NY.

[2]Jan Diehl: Arlington Heights, IL.

[3]Chris DeTomasi: Lake Zurich, IL.

[4]*Sew News*, October 1987, p. 51.

[5]Karen Henderson, as cited by Ruth G. Shephard, "Tips & Techniques," *Country Needlecraft*, May/June 1989, p. 4.

[6]Dorothy Simms: Clio, MI.

[7]Julie Hussar: Linden, MI.

[8]Pat Hardy and Marian Meyers, in *Quilter's Ranch Dispatch*, January/February 1987, p. 7.

INDEX

NOTES:

NOTES:

NOTES: